Beginning Microsoft Word Business Documents

From Novice to Professional

James J. Marshall

Apress®

Beginning Microsoft Word Business Documents

Copyright © 2006 by James J. Marshall

ISBN-13 (pbk): 978-1-59059-728-6

ISBN-10 (pbk): 1-59059-728-1

Printed and bound in the United States of America 9 8 7 6 5 4 3 2 1

Lead Editor: Jim Sumser
Technical Reviewer: Carlos Castillo
Editorial Board: Steve Anglin, Ewan Buckingham, Gary Cornell, Jason Gilmore, Jonathan Gennick, Jonathan Hassell, James Huddleston, Chris Mills, Matthew Moodie, Dominic Shakeshaft, Jim Sumser, Keir Thomas, Matt Wade
Project Manager: Richard Dal Porto
Copy Edit Manager: Nicole LeClerc
Copy Editor: Ami Knox
Assistant Production Director: Kari Brooks-Copony
Production Editor: Lori Bring
Compositor: Susan Glinert
Proofreader: Dan Shaw
Indexer: Carol Burbo
Cover Designer: Kurt Krames
Manufacturing Director: Tom Debolski

Distributed to the book trade worldwide by Springer-Verlag New York, Inc., 233 Spring Street, 6th Floor, New York, NY 10013. Phone 1-800-SPRINGER, fax 201-348-4505, e-mail orders-ny@springer-sbm.com, or visit http://www.springeronline.com.

For information on translations, please contact Apress directly at 2560 Ninth Street, Suite 219, Berkeley, CA 94710. Phone 510-549-5930, fax 510-549-5939, e-mail info@apress.com, or visit http://www.apress.com.

Contents at a Glance

Contents

About the Author

JAMES J. MARSHALL is a copywriter and personal technology writer living in the Southwest. He currently writes the content for About.com's word processing site, in addition to working on many other projects. For more information about the author and book, please visit his web site at `http://jamesjmarshall.com`.

Acknowledgments

I would like to thank the team at Apress, whose dedication and professionalism made this book possible. Working with you has been a pleasure.

Thank you Hannah, Michael, and Monica for your lasting friendships and for listening to my plights and gripes about deadlines and long hours.

And, of course, many thanks to P. for her loyal companionship.

Introduction

Thank you for your interest in this book. My goal in writing this book is to help you create professional documents in Microsoft Word with a minimum of effort.

The step-by-step instructions will show you everything you need to know about creating business documents in an easy-to-follow manner.

Who Should Read This Book

This book is designed for intermediate Word users or anyone who wants to increase their Word skills. Because the book is geared specifically to business documents, it is best suited for people who must create these documents on a regular or frequent basis.

How to Use This Book

Each chapter shows you how to create a certain type of document or a related type of document.

I recommend that all readers familiarize themselves with Chapter 1, which lays the groundwork for the subsequent chapters. From there, you can read any chapter that suits your needs.

Like Chapter 1, Chapters 9 and 10 will be pertinent to many readers. These chapters will help readers who are working on unwieldy documents or who would like to increase their efficiency by automating tasks.

Within each chapter, you will find tips, notes, and cautions. These expand on topics discussed in the body of the chapter. They offer advice for getting the most out of the features or for avoiding problems with certain features.

Additionally, sidebars offer expanded explanations and advice for certain features. Together these will help you get the most out of Word by avoiding the program's potential pitfalls.

Finally, sample documents for each chapter are available at the Apress web site (http://www.apress.com). You can download these documents and alter them to suit your needs.

What You'll Find in This Book

Following is a chapter-by-chapter breakdown of this book:

- *Chapter 1, Planning and Creating a Document:* Every reader should take a look at this chapter, as it covers everything you need to know about creating a basic document in Word. This document serves as the basis for every document created in the subsequent chapters. What's more, you can use this basic document to create any type of document.

- *Chapter 2, Creating a Business Plan:* If your company is a new startup, a business plan is essential, as it will help investors assess the viability of the business. This chapter guides you through the process of creating such a document.

- *Chapter 3, Creating Marketing Brochures and Newsletters:* This chapter shows you how to use the advanced formatting features required for marketing brochures and newsletters.

- *Chapter 4, Creating Forms for Printing or Distributing Electronically:* If you need a form to gather information electronically, read this chapter. It shows you how to use Word's form tools to get the job done. It's also handy for creating printed forms, such as job applications.

- *Chapter 5, Creating Legal Documents:* There are a variety of different legal filings, and the formatting will vary from court to court. However, this chapter shows you formatting elements you can use with any type of legal filing.

- *Chapter 6, Creating Data Sheets:* If you're creating a data sheet, it may seem like you need to use a desktop publishing program to accomplish a clean layout. That is not the case. You can accomplish the task quite easily in Word, and this chapter shows you how.

- *Chapter 7, Creating Organization Charts:* Rather than use Word's Drawing Objects to create a chart of a company's structure, use the Organization Chart feature. You can create a customized organization chart in a snap!

- *Chapter 8, Creating a Grant or Business Proposal:* Grants and business proposals are essential to most businesses and nonprofit organizations. When asking for a grant or project, correct formatting is crucial, as it will make your business appear more professional and competent. This chapter shows you everything you need to know.

- *Chapter 9, Automating Document Creation*: Once you've created your document, chances are you will be creating more in the future. Or, you may want to create multiple, yet differing, copies all at once. This chapter will help you do that. Learn how to use Mail Merge and other features to automate the document creation process.

- *Chapter 10, Working with Large Documents*: Finally, Chapter 10 will give you advice for working with very long documents. In a business environment, this is a must read. It also shows you how to use tools specially designed for use in a collaborative environment.

■ ■ ■

CHAPTER 1

Planning and Creating a Document

If you are creating a document with many different sections and a variety of information, the formatting can become an intricate process. But by planning the document before you start creating it, you will simplify the process.

This chapter will show you how to plan and create a basic document. The subsequent chapters will take you through the steps of customizing the basic document to create specific types of business documents.

Getting Started with Word's Outline View

With a multipart document, it's best to start with an outline, as it will allow you to organize the different parts of the document. You will also see at a glance the sections you are including, so you won't inadvertently omit a portion of the document.

More importantly, outlines are particularly helpful when you need to include a table of contents with your document. The outline levels will help you create a table of contents that updates automatically as the document evolves.

With Word's Outline view, you can create an outline with ease. To switch to Outline view, click the View menu and select Outline. The Outline view differs substantially from other document views. You will also notice that the Outlining toolbar appears below the Standard and Formatting toolbars, as shown in Figure 1-1. It contains a number of options that will help you work with your outline.

Note When you change document views, you may not see certain elements of your document. Also, with the exception of Print Layout view, the document views do not accurately represent how your finished document will appear. Keep this in mind as you work. If you need to gauge how your finished document will look, you can toggle back and forth between document views. You can do this via the View menu or the view buttons in the lower left of the Word window. The Print Preview button on the Standard toolbar also shows you how your document will look.

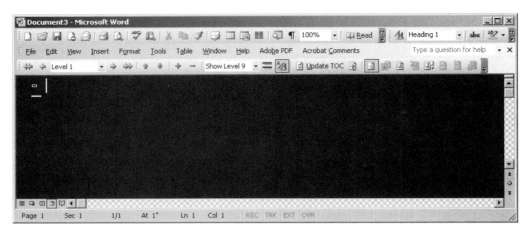

Figure 1-1. *Word's Outline view*

In Outline view, enter each section heading on a new line. You should also enter headings for the subsections. Notice that a small minus symbol appears in the left margin of each line.

Once you have entered the section headings and subsection headings, you are ready to assign each heading a level. Think of it as a standard outline, even though you might not use Roman numerals, numbers, and letters.

By default, Word assigns each line to Level 1. You will probably find that most of the sections of your document remain at Level 1. However, some sections will require subsections. So you will need to move the sections to a lower level.

There are several ways to change a heading level, the easiest being to place the cursor at the beginning of the heading and then use the Tab key to change the level. Press the Tab key once to lower the heading one level. You will notice that the minus sign in the left margin on the preceding level changes to a plus sign, as Figure 1-2 illustrates.

Tip Should you need to promote a heading up a level, press Shift+Tab to move it. The headings subordinate to the heading you move will not move automatically. If you want the subheadings to maintain the same relative position, use the plus sign in the left margin. Click it to highlight the level and its subordinate levels. When you change the level, the relative position of the other levels also changes.

If you need to change the order of one of the headings, click the plus or minus sign in the margin. Then drag it to the correct location. A dotted line will show you the new location for the heading. When you move a level, you will also move the sublevels.

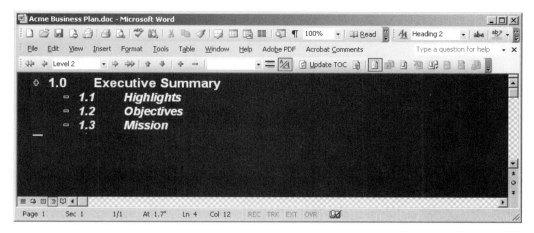

Figure 1-2. *Showing sublevels in Outline view*

■**Note** When you switch to Print Layout view, you will notice that Word has automatically applied formatting to your document. This is normal. Word uses the heading styles incorporated in the Normal.dot template, the template upon which all blank documents are based. If you do not want to use the default styles, don't worry. The styles can be altered later when you format the document.

■**Tip** When working in Outline view, you can expand or collapse a portion of your outline by double-clicking the plus sign in the margin. If you want to collapse your entire outline, use the Outlining toolbar. The Show Level drop-down box, shown in Figure 1-3, allows you to select the levels you would like to view. You can select Levels 1 through 9, or you can opt to show all levels.

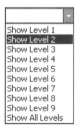

Figure 1-3. *The Show Level drop-down box on the Outlining toolbar*

Entering the Main Body Text

Now you are ready for creating the main document. At this stage, you should enter text only. You will insert charts, tables, graphs, and other document elements later.

Also, avoid applying any formatting to the document. This includes bold, italics, and underline. You do not want to use indentation yet, nor should you use the Tab key to indent text.

Right now, your primary concern is to enter the text data in your document. You will apply formatting to paragraphs and text in one stage. This ensures that you achieve clean, consistent formatting throughout the document. Use Word's style feature to apply the formatting, so Word will not retain manually applied formats.

Specifying Page Setup

Now you are ready to specify the page setup for the entire document. You may decide later to alter the page setup in specific parts of your document, or you may already know that the page setup will differ in certain areas. This is okay. For now, you are setting the predominant page layout for your document.

Access the Page Setup dialog box by clicking File ➤ Page Setup. Click the Margins tab to open the settings for the margins, as shown in Figure 1-4.

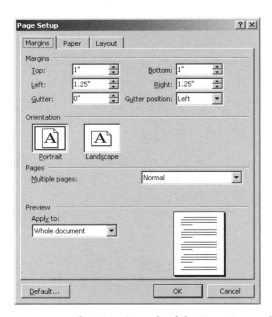

Figure 1-4. *The Margins tab of the Page Setup dialog box*

The default settings for the Normal.dot template are 1 inch at the top and bottom of the page and 1.25 inches at either side of the page. In most situations, these settings are appropriate for documents. However, if you plan to bind the document, for example, you may want to increase the margins. This ensures that the binding will not obstruct any of the printing.

■Caution Avoid increasing the margins without a good reason, such as accommodating a binding. Otherwise, the margins will become distracting, and your document may look insubstantial. Similarly, do not decrease the margins to fit more on the page. This will make the document look cramped and difficult to read.

If you plan to add a header and footer, take that into consideration. Word will place the header and footer outside the margins you specify. You should also consider any footnotes you have added to the document.

The default page orientation is portrait, but you can change it to landscape. Also, check that the drop-down box labeled Pages reads Normal. In the drop-down box labeled Apply to, select Whole document.

Next, click the Paper tab in the Page Setup dialog box (see Figure 1-5). In the Paper size section, use the drop-down box to specify the paper size. Letter size will be most common.

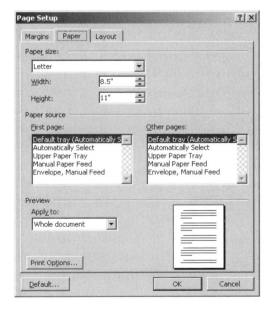

Figure 1-5. *The Paper tab of the Page Setup dialog box*

Use the boxes in the Paper source section to specify the printer's paper tray(s) for the first page of the document and for the subsequent pages. In the Preview section, opt to apply the changes to the whole document.

Click the Print Options button to review the settings in the Print dialog box, as shown in Figure 1-6. Deselect Draft output if it has been selected. Select Update fields. This tells Word to check that the fields are current when the document prints. Similarly, select Update links. You should also select Drawing objects.

Figure 1-6. *The Print dialog box*

Once you have made your selections, click OK.

On the Layout tab, shown in Figure 1-7, check the document's vertical alignment. In most cases, you'll want the text aligned to the top of the page, so select Top in the drop-down box. Once again, opt to apply the changes to the whole document, and click OK.

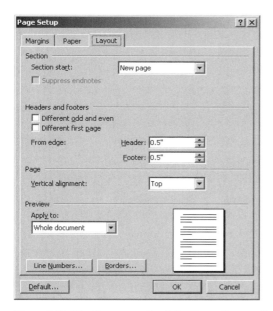

Figure 1-7. *The Layout tab of the Page Setup dialog box*

Formatting Your Document with Styles

When you're applying styles to your document, you have several tools that will help you. First, there is the Styles and Formatting task pane. To open it, click View ➤ Task Pane (or press Ctrl+F1). The task pane will appear in the right side of the Word window. Click the arrow at the top of the task pane and select Styles and Formatting. To open the Styles and Formatting task pane faster, simply click the Styles and Formatting button on the Formatting toolbar.

The Styles and Formatting task pane provides an easy way to create and apply styles. Once you select the portion of your document you would like to format, simply click a style in the task pane. Conveniently, the task pane identifies the section's current style, as shown in Figure 1-8.

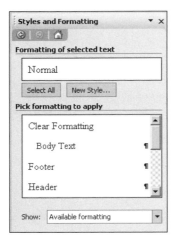

Figure 1-8. *The Styles and Formatting task pane showing the current style*

The Formatting toolbar also provides an easy way to check a selection's style and to apply styles. Simply select a portion of your document and use the Style drop-down box, shown in Figure 1-9, to apply a style. When you select a portion of your document, its style will appear in the Style box.

Figure 1-9. *The Style box on the Formatting toolbar*

You can also view applied styles at a glance by activating the Styles area. By default, Word hides the Styles area. But to activate it, click Tools ➤ Options and open the View tab, shown in Figure 1-10. On the bottom of the tab, use the controls in the box labeled Style area width to specify the width for the Styles area. Click OK.

The Styles area, shown in Figure 1-11, will appear along the left side of the window. A thin frame separates the Styles area from the rest of the document. You can click and drag the frame to increase or decrease the size of the Styles area.

■**Note** The Styles area does have limitations. First, you can only display it in Outline or Normal view. Second, it only shows styles applied to paragraphs. The Styles area will not display styles you apply to characters or portions of a paragraph. It is a handy feature, nonetheless.

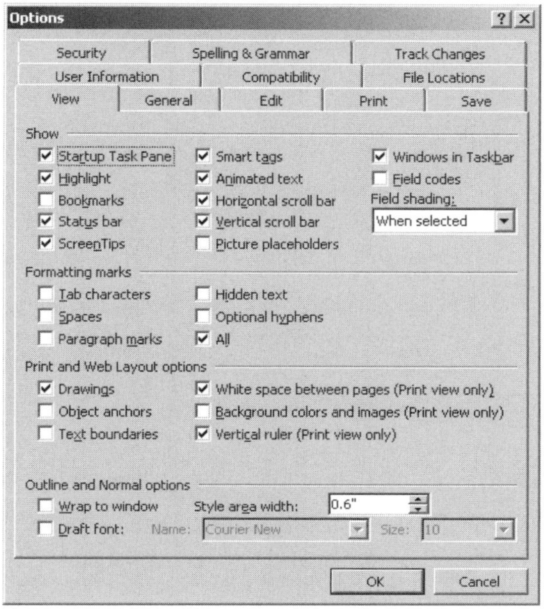

Figure 1-10. *The View tab of the Options dialog box*

Figure 1-11. *The Styles area*

You can also use the Styles area to change a paragraph's style. Double-click the style name in the Styles area. In the Style dialog box, shown in Figure 1-12, select the new style and then click Apply.

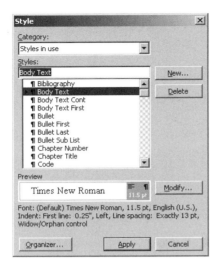

Figure 1-12. *The Style dialog box*

Word includes a variety of styles for you to use. But you may want to create your own styles. Fortunately, creating a style is not as difficult as you would assume.

The easiest way to create a style is to base it on a portion of the document. First, apply the formats you want to include in the style to part of your document. Paragraph styles can include character formatting such as bold, italics, underline, font color, and font size. Additionally, you can include alignment, margins, line spacing, and indents.

Once you have formatted the text, you have three options for defining the style. First, you can click in the Style box on the Formatting toolbar and type a name for the style. Or, in the Styles and Formatting task pane, click the New Style button. Type a name for the style in the Name box and click OK (see Figure 1-13). Lastly, you can use the Styles area. Double-click the style name next to the formatted paragraph. In the Style dialog box, click New. Type a name for the style in the Name box and click OK.

You can also create a style by specifying the formatting manually in the New Style dialog box. To access the New Style dialog box, click the New Style button in the Styles and Formatting task pane.

Enter a name for the style in the box labeled Name. Next, specify the type of style in the Style type box. You can select Paragraph, Character, Table, or List. Your choices will vary based on the type of style you create.

Use the controls to specify the formats to include in the style. If you don't see the options you need, click the Format button. A list pops up with more formatting options (see Figure 1-14). The preview area shows you how the style will look.

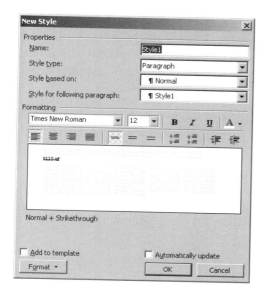

Figure 1-13. *The New Style dialog box*

Figure 1-14. *The Format list in the New Style dialog box*

You can tell Word to update the style when you make changes to text formatted with the style. Simply select Automatically update. When you have finalized your choices, click OK.

You can also create a new style based on an existing style. In the New Style dialog box, select the style you want to use in the drop-down list labeled Style based on.

■**Caution** If you modify a base style, Word will update all styles you created from the base style. To avoid this, select (no style) in the drop-down list box labeled Style based on in the New Style dialog box.

There is a good chance you will decide to modify a style you created. To do this, you need to access the Modify Style dialog box, as shown in Figure 1-15. In the Styles and Formatting task pane, hold the mouse over the style you would like to modify. Click the arrow that appears and select Modify. The Modify Style dialog box, which is similar to the New Style dialog box, will open.

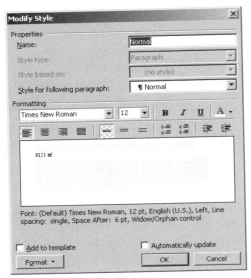

Figure 1-15. *The Modify Style dialog box is similar to the New Style dialog box.*

Alternatively, you can modify a style by formatting a portion of your document with the formats you would like to include in the style. Then hold the mouse over the style you would like to modify in the Styles and Formatting task pane. Click the arrow that appears and select Update to Match Selection.

■**Tip** If you want to change all instances of a particular style, select a portion of the document formatted with the style. In the Styles and Formatting task pane, click the Select All button. Then click the new style you would like to apply. Also, you can delete all text formatted with the selected style by pressing Delete or Backspace.

Saving Your Document As a Template

Once you have completed your document, you may decide to save it as a template. That way, you can base future documents on the one you just created. Word will automatically create a new document based on the template, so you won't need to worry about overwriting the document.

The template will help you cut down on the time it takes you to create future documents, because it will retain the options you specified for page setup, headers and footers, and the like. Additionally, the template will include the styles you personalized.

Templates are particularly handy in multiuser environments. With templates, other people in your office will be able to create documents that contain formatting consistent with the one you've created.

To save your document as a template, click File ➤ Save As. In the box labeled File Name, give your template an easily recognizable name. In the box labeled Save as type, select Document Template.

Word automatically opens the default save location for templates. In Word 2003, this location is C:\Documents and Settings\username\Application Data\Microsoft\Templates.

■**Note** You must save the template in this location if you want to access it from the Templates dialog box. However, you can save it on removable media or anywhere on your hard drive.You may want to save it on a CD-ROM for easy distribution.

If you wish to save your template in a location other than the default template location, use the address bar to navigate to the folder of your choice. Once you have made your selections, click Save.

■■■

CHAPTER 2

Creating a Business Plan

The many different sections and variety of information contained in a business plan make its formatting an intricate process. But by planning the document before you start creating it, you will simplify the process.

A sample business plan is available with the downloads for this book at the Apress web site (http://www.apress.com).

Getting Started with Word's Outline View

With a multipart document, it is best to start with an outline, which will allow you to organize the different parts of the document. You will also see at a glance the sections you are including, so you won't inadvertently omit a portion of the document.

More importantly, outlines are particularly helpful when you need to include a table of contents with your document. The outline levels will help you create a table of contents that updates automatically as the document evolves.

With Word's Outline view, you can create an outline with ease. To switch to Outline view, shown in Figure 2-1, click the View menu and select Outline. The Outline view differs substantially from other document views. You will also notice that the Outlining toolbar appears below the Standard and Formatting toolbars. It contains a number of options that will help you work with your outline.

■**Note** When you change document views, you may not see certain elements of your document. Also, with the exception of Print Layout view, the document views do not accurately represent how your finished document will appear. Keep this in mind as you work. If you need to gauge how your finished document will look, you can toggle back and forth between document views. You can do this via the View menu or the view buttons in the lower left of the Word window. The Print Preview button on the Standard toolbar also shows you how your document will look.

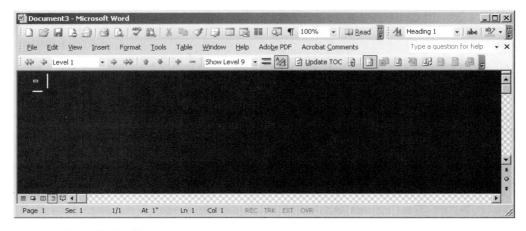

Figure 2-1. *Word's Outline view*

In Outline view, enter each section heading on a new line. You should also enter headings for the subsections. Notice that a small minus sign appears in the left margin of each line.

Once you have entered the section headings and subsection headings, you are ready to assign each heading a level. Think of it as a standard outline, even though you might not use Roman numerals, numbers, and letters.

By default, Word assigns each line to Level 1. You will probably find that most of the sections of your business plan remain at Level 1. However, some sections will require subsections. So you will need to move the sections to a lower level.

There are several ways to change a heading level. The easiest way to change a heading level is to place the cursor at the beginning of the heading. Then use the Tab key to change the level. Press the Tab key once to lower the heading one level. You will notice that the minus sign in the left margin on the preceding level changes to a plus sign, as you can see in Figure 2-2.

Should you need to promote a heading up a level, press Shift+Tab to move it.

■**Note** When you switch to Print Layout view, you will notice that Word has automatically applied formatting to your document. This is normal. Word uses the heading styles incorporated in the Normal.dot template, the template upon which all blank documents are based. If you do not want to use the default styles, don't worry. The styles can be altered later when you format the document.

The headings subordinate to the heading you move will not move automatically. If you want the subheadings to maintain the same relative position, use the plus sign in the left margin. Click it to highlight the level and its subordinate levels. When you change the level, the relative position of the other levels also changes (see Figure 2-3).

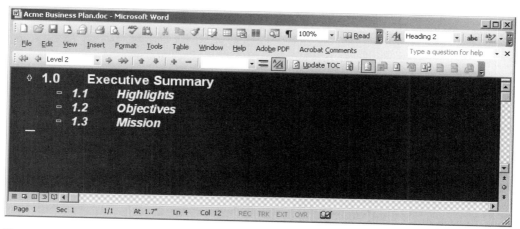

Figure 2-2. *Showing sublevels in Outline view*

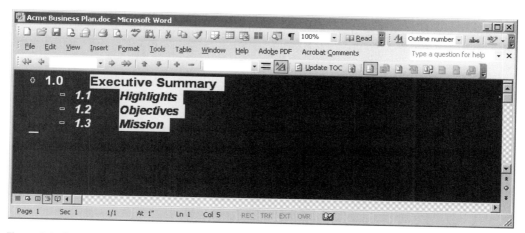

Figure 2-3. *Several outline levels selected*

■Tip When working in Outline view, you can expand or collapse a portion of your outline by double-clicking the plus sign in the margin. If you want to collapse your entire outline, use the Outlining toolbar. The Show Level drop-down box allows you to select the levels you would like to view. You can select levels 1 through 9, or you can opt to show all levels, as you see in Figure 2-4.

If you need to change the order of one of the headings, click the plus or minus sign in the margin. Then drag it to the correct location. When you move a level, you will also move the sublevels.

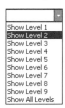

Figure 2-4. *The Show Level drop-down box on the Outlining toolbar*

Creating a Table of Contents

Once you have created your outline, you're ready for the table of contents. You may find it counterintuitive to create the table of contents before the rest of the document. When you create a table of contents manually, it makes sense to insert it when the document is finalized. That way, you don't need to worry about updating page numbers.

Word will create a table of contents automatically. By using this feature, you will avoid the problems associated with creating one manually. First, Word uses the headings you entered in Outline view to create the table of contents. You won't need to waste time entering the information a second time.

Word also makes it easy to format the table, providing several predefined options. But, best of all, Word will automatically update the page numbering for you. So, as your document grows in length, the table of contents will reflect the changes.

■**Tip** You may still wonder why it makes sense to create the table of contents now. The answer is simple. You can use the table of contents to navigate through your document because it is linked to the sections of the business plan. Simply hold the mouse pointer over one of the entries in the table of contents, then hold the Ctrl key and click the mouse. Word takes you to that section of your document.

To insert your table of contents, place the cursor at the beginning of the first line of your outline. Then click Insert ➤ Reference ➤ Index and Tables.

The Index and Tables dialog box, shown in Figure 2-5, will open. Open the Table of Contents tab.

The Print Preview box will show you how the table of contents will appear in final form. Word will not show the actual headings in the Print Preview box. Rather, it shows the position of the different heading levels, substituting "Heading 1," "Heading 2," and so forth in place of headings.

Word has six predefined formats for you to choose. You can also opt to apply text formatting from the document template, which allows you to base the formatting on styles you specify.

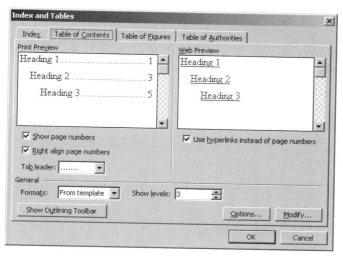

Figure 2-5. *The Table of Contents tab on the Index and Tables dialog box*

The predefined formats will save you some time. However, they may not be appropriate for a business plan. If you decide to use one, opt for the Classic format.

You are also able to change certain elements in the table of contents. You can alter the appearance of page numbers and leader lines and select how many levels the table of contents will contain.

With a professional document such as a business plan, you should emphasize function over form. So design the table of contents with readability in mind.

Page numbers are a necessity, so make sure to select Show page numbers. You probably also want to select Right align page numbers. This will give the table a clean, organized look.

If you align the page numbers along the right margin, you will do well to add tab leader lines. These lines will guide the reader's eye to the correct page number. Of course, Word provides a few different choices for how the leader lines appear. A dotted leader line is both unobtrusive and effective. Use the drop-down box to select the style you want.

Note Switching between predefined formats may change the other options in the dialog box. So if you make a change, don't forget to reselect any options that have changed.

Finally, use the Show levels drop-down box to select how many heading levels to show. Moderation is best. However, you want your reader to find the relevant section easily.

When you've specified the options for the table, click OK. Your table of contents appears at the top of the document, above the document outline.

If you switch to Print Layout view, you will notice that the table of contents is on the same page as the outline. You will want to insert a page break between the table of contents and the rest of the business plan.

To insert a page break, position the cursor at the end of the table of contents. Click Insert ➤ Break. In the Break dialog box, shown in Figure 2-6, select Page break and click OK. This ensures that the business plan will begin on a new page. The break will not appear in Outline view.

Figure 2-6. *The Break dialog box*

As you work on the business plan, Word may not update the page numbers or headings in the table of contents. This is normal. Word will make the appropriate changes when you print the document.

If it is important to you that the table of contents be updated as you work, you can tell Word to update it. On the Outlining toolbar, click Update TOC. The Update Table of Contents dialog box appears, as shown in Figure 2-7.

Figure 2-7. *The Update Table of Contents dialog box*

You will have two choices on what to update. Choose Update page numbers only if you want to update only the page numbers. If you've made changes to the headings, select Update entire table. Click OK.

Adding a Cover Page

Next you should create a cover page for your business plan. Position the cursor at the beginning of the first line of your outline. Enter the information you would like to appear on the cover page. Each line on the cover page should appear on its own line in Outline view.

Once you have entered the information for the cover page, you need to assign it to the correct level in the outline. Highlight the cover page information. Then on the Outlining toolbar, click the Outline Level drop-down box. Click Body text.

Finally, you want to make sure the cover page information appears on its own page. Position the cursor at the end of the final line of the cover page. Click Insert ➤ Break. In the Break dialog box, select Page break and click OK. You will not see the page break in Outline view.

Entering the Main Body Text

Now you are ready for the main document. At this stage, you should enter text only. You will insert your charts, tables, and graphs later.

Also, avoid applying any formatting to the document. This includes bold, italics, and underline. You do not want to use indentation yet, nor should you use the Tab key to indent text.

Right now, your primary concern is to enter the text data in your business plan. You will apply formatting to paragraphs and text in one stage. This ensures that you achieve clean, consistent formatting throughout the business plan. Use Word's Styles feature to apply the formatting, so Word will not retain manually applied formats.

Citing Sources with Footnotes

If you cite outside sources in your business plan, it is important to credit them properly with footnotes. Word automates the process so the numbering is always correct. If you make changes to the document, you don't need to worry about the placement of the footnotes.

To insert a footnote, place the cursor where you want to position the footnote mark. Then click Insert ➤ Reference ➤ Footnote. In the Location section in the Footnote and Endnote dialog box, select Footnotes and specify Bottom of page, as shown in Figure 2-8. Click Insert.

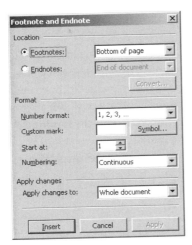

Figure 2-8. *The Footnote and Endnote dialog box*

Word will insert the footnote mark at the selected location and take you to the footnote section at the bottom of the page (see Figure 2-9). There, you can enter the footnote text. Add formatting as you would for any other portion of your document.

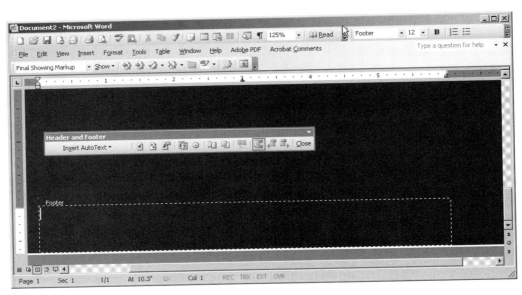

Figure 2-9. *The Footnote area in the main document*

Specifying Page Setup

Now you are ready to specify the page setup for the entire document. You may decide later to alter the page setup in specific parts of your business plan. Or you may already know that the page setup will differ in certain areas. That is okay. For now, you are setting the predominant page layout for your business plan.

Access the Page Setup dialog box by clicking File ➤ Page Setup. Click the Margins tab to open the settings for the margins, as shown in Figure 2-10.

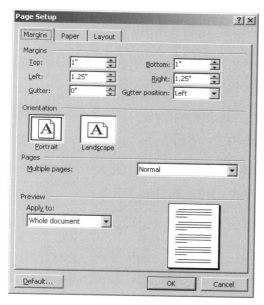

Figure 2-10. *The Margins tab of the Page Setup dialog box*

The default settings for the Normal.dot template are 1 inch at the top and bottom of the page and 1.25 inches at either side of the page. In most situations, these settings are appropriate for a business plan. However, if you plan to bind the business plan, you may want to increase the left margin by .25 inch. This ensures that the binding will not obstruct any of the printing.

■**Caution** Avoid increasing the margins without a good reason, such as accommodating a binding. Otherwise, the margins will become distracting, and your business plan may look insubstantial. Similarly, do not decrease the margins to fit more on the page. This will make the business plan look cramped and difficult to read.

If you plan to add a header and footer, take that into consideration. Word will place the header and footer outside the margins you specify. You should also consider any footnotes you have added to the document.

The page orientation should be portrait. Also, check that the drop-down box labeled Pages reads Normal. The other options are not appropriate for a business plan. In the drop-down box labeled Apply to, select Whole document.

Next click the Paper tab in the Page Setup dialog box. In the Paper size section, shown in Figure 2-11, use the drop-down box to specify the paper size. It should be Letter size, unless you must submit your business plan on A4 or A6 paper.

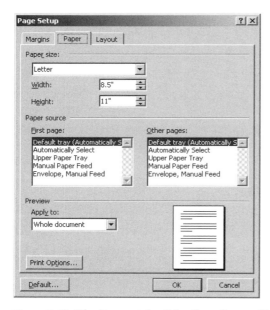

Figure 2-11. *The Paper tab of the Page Setup dialog box*

Use the boxes in the Paper source section to specify the printer's paper tray(s) for the first page of the business plan and for the subsequent pages. In the Preview section, opt to apply the changes to the whole document.

Click the Print Options button to review the settings, as shown in Figure 2-12. Deselect Draft output if it has been selected. Select Update fields. This tells Word to check that the fields are current when the document prints. Similarly, select Update links. You should also select Drawing objects.

Once you have made your selections, click OK.

On the Layout tab, check the document's vertical alignment, as shown in Figure 2-13. You want the text aligned to the top of the page, so select Top in the drop-down box. Once again, opt to apply the changes to the whole document. Click OK.

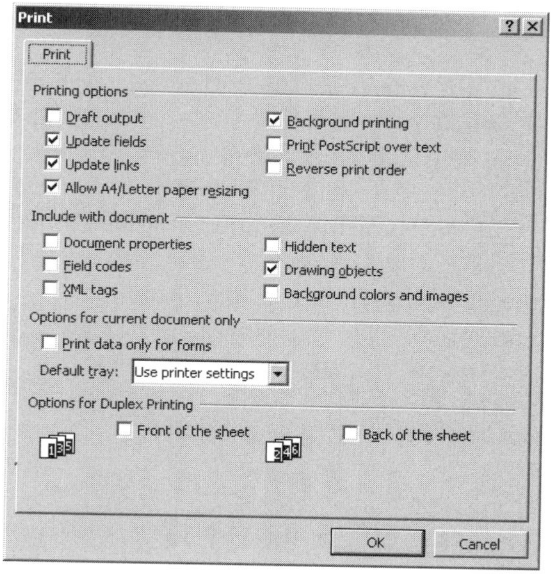

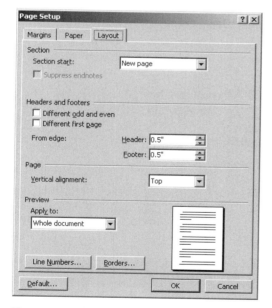

Figure 2-12. *The Print dialog box*

Figure 2-13. *The Layout tab of the Page Setup dialog box*

Formatting Your Business Plan with Styles

When you're applying styles to your document, you have several tools that will help you. First, there is the Styles and Formatting task pane. To open it, click View ➤ Task Pane (or press Ctrl+F1). The task pane will appear in the right side of the Word window. Click the arrow at the top of the task pane and select Styles and Formatting. To open the Styles and Formatting task pane faster, simply click the Styles and Formatting button on the Formatting toolbar.

The Styles and Formatting task pane provides an easy way to create and apply styles. Once you select the portion of your document you would like to format, simply click a style in the task pane. Conveniently, the task pane identifies the section's current style, as you see in Figure 2-14.

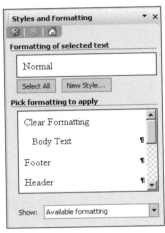

Figure 2-14. *The Styles and Formatting task pane showing the current style*

The Formatting toolbar also provides an easy way to check a selection's style and to apply styles. Simply select a portion of your document and use the Style drop-down box to apply a style (see Figure 2-15). When you select a portion of your document, its style will appear in the Style box.

Figure 2-15. *The Style box on the Formatting toolbar*

You can also view applied styles at a glance by activating the Styles area. By default, Word hides the Styles area. But to activate it, click Tools ➤ Options and open the View tab, as shown in Figure 2-16. On the bottom of the tab, use the controls in the box labeled Style area width to specify the width for the Styles area. Click OK.

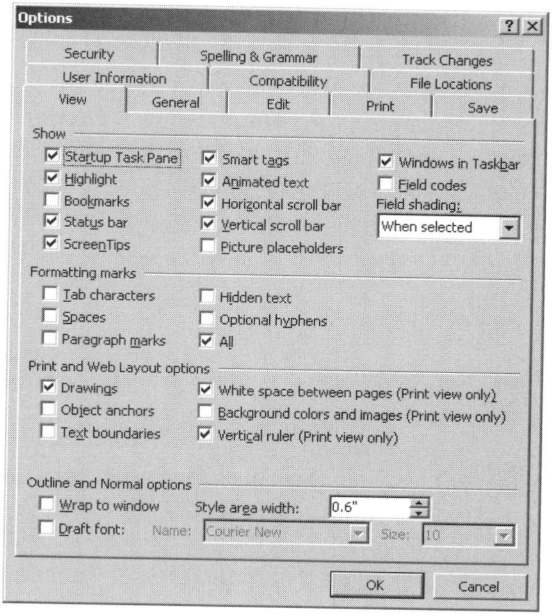

Figure 2-16. *The View tab of the Options dialog box*

The Styles area will appear along the left side of the window, as you see in Figure 2-17. A thin frame separates the Styles area from the rest of the document. You can click and drag the frame to increase or decrease the size of the Styles area.

Figure 2-17. *The Styles area*

■**Note** The Styles area does have limitations. First, you can only display it in Outline or Normal view. Second, it only shows styles applied to paragraphs. The Styles area will not display styles you apply to characters or portions of a paragraph. It is a handy feature, nonetheless.

You can also use the Styles area to change a paragraph's style. Double-click the style name in the Styles area. In the Style dialog box, shown in Figure 2-18, select the new style and then click apply.

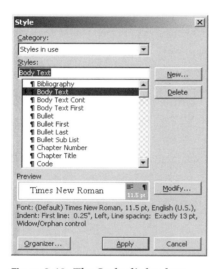

Figure 2-18. *The Style dialog box*

Word includes a variety of styles for you to use. But you may want to create your own styles. Fortunately, creating a style is not as difficult as you would assume.

The easiest way to create a style is to base it on a portion of the document. First, apply the formats you want to include in the style to part of your document. Paragraph styles can include character formatting such as bold, italics, underline, font color, and font size. Additionally, you can include alignment, margins, line spacing, and indents.

Once you have formatted the text, you have three options for defining the style. First, you can click in the Styles box on the Formatting toolbar and type a name for the style. Or, in the Styles and Formatting task pane, click the New Style button. Type a name for the style in the Name box, as shown in Figure 2-19, and click OK. Lastly, you can use the Styles area. Double-click the style name next to the formatted paragraph. In the Style dialog box, click New. Type a name for the style in the Name box and click OK.

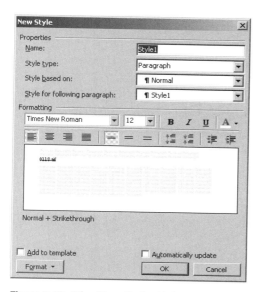

Figure 2-19. *The New Style dialog box*

You can also create a style by specifying the formatting manually in the New Style dialog box. To access the New Style dialog box, click the New Style button on the Styles and Formatting task pane.

Enter a name for the style in the box labeled Name. Next specify the type of style in the Style type box. You can select Paragraph, Character, Table, or List. Your choices will vary based on the type of style you create.

Use the controls to specify the formats to include in the style. If you don't see the options you need, click the Format button. A list pops up with more formatting options (see Figure 2-20). The preview area shows you how the style will look.

Figure 2-20. *The Format list on the New Style dialog box*

You can tell Word to update the style when you make changes to text formatted with the style. Simply select Automatically update. When you have finalized your choices, click OK.

You can also create a new style based on an existing style. In the New Style dialog box, select the style you want to use in the drop-down list labeled Style based on.

■**Caution**   If you modify a base style, Word will update all styles you created from the base style. To avoid this, select (no style) in the drop-down list box labeled Style based on in the New Style dialog box.

There is a good chance you will decide to modify a style you created. To do this, you need to access the Modify Style dialog box, as shown in Figure 2-21. In the Styles and Formatting task pane, hold the mouse over the style you would like to modify. Click the arrow that appears and select Modify. The Modify Style dialog box, which is similar to the New Style dialog box, will open.

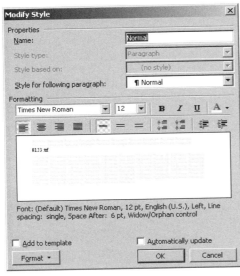

Figure 2-21. *The Modify Style dialog box is similar to the New Style dialog box.*

Alternatively, you can modify a style by formatting a portion of your document with the formats you would like to include in the style. Then hold the mouse over the style you would like to modify in the Styles and Formatting task pane. Click the arrow that appears and select Update to Match Selection.

Tip If you want to change all instances of a particular style, select a portion of the document formatted with the style. In the Styles and Formatting task pane, click the Select All button. Then click the new style you would like to apply. Also, you can delete all text formatted with the selected style by pressing Delete or Backspace.

Inserting a Table

Tables will play an important role in your business plan. Use tables to organize data in balance sheets, sales projections, and other financials.

The easiest way for you to create a table in Word is to use the Insert Table button on the Standard toolbar.

Position the cursor where you would like the table. Then click the Insert Table button. Use the drop-down grid to select the number of rows and columns for the table, as shown in Figure 2-22. When you release the mouse, Word inserts the table at the appropriate location in your document.

Figure 2-22. *Using the Insert Table button to create a table*

As Figure 2-23 illustrates, you will notice that tables you create with this method span the entire width of the document, no matter how many columns they contain.

For more control over your columns, use the Insert Table dialog box. It allows you to specify a number of different formatting options for your table.

To access the Insert Table dialog box, place the cursor where you would like to position the table. Then click Table ➤ Insert ➤ Table. In the Insert Table dialog box, specify the number of columns and rows you would like the table to contain, as shown in Figure 2-24. You can also set options for the column width. By default, Word automatically sets the width of the columns. However, you can use the Fixed column width box to specify the width of the columns in inches. Or, you can have Word automatically fit the table to the window or table contents by selecting one of the AutoFit options.

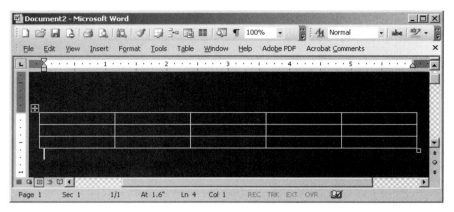

Figure 2-23. *A table created with the Insert Table button*

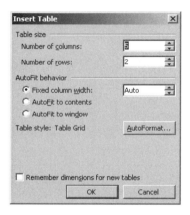

Figure 2-24. *The Insert Table dialog box*

Notice the AutoFormat button on the Insert Table dialog box. This opens a dialog box that allows you to specify predetermined formats to the table. In the Table AutoFormat dialog box, shown in Figure 2-25, you first select a table style. Word displays the table formatting in the Preview box. At the bottom of the dialog box, you can use the selections to add or remove formatting from specific rows and columns. When you're done, click OK. Then click OK in the Insert Table dialog box.

To enter data in the table, simply click in a cell and begin typing.

If you decide you want to add more rows or columns to your table, you can do so quite easily. To add a row, click to the left of the row below which you would like to add a new row. Once the row is selected, the Insert Table button on the Standard toolbar changes to the Insert Rows button, as you see in Figure 2-26.

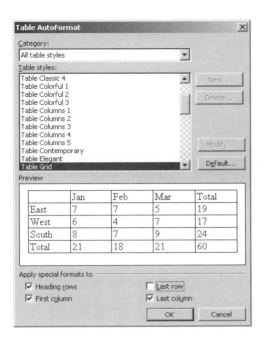

Figure 2-25. *The Table AutoFormat dialog box*

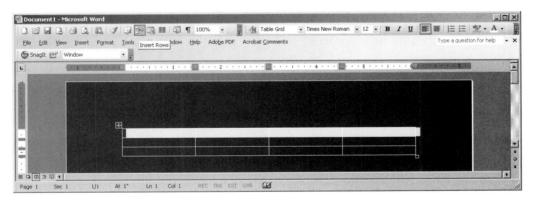

Figure 2-26. *Adding a row to a table*

To add a column, click the border above the column beside which you would like to insert an additional column. The Insert Table button on the Standard toolbar changes to the Insert Columns button. Word inserts the column to the left of the selected column (see Figure 2-27).

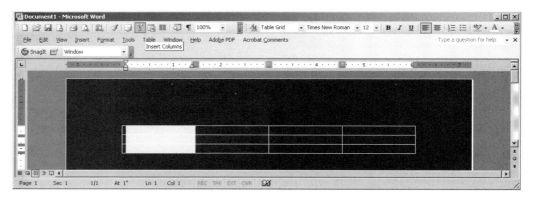

Figure 2-27. *Adding a column to a table*

■**Tip**   For more flexibility in choosing where to insert rows and columns, use the Insert submenu on the Table menu instead of the toolbar buttons.

To remove rows or columns, select the row or column you would like to delete. Then click Table ➤ Delete and specify what to delete.

Modifying a Table's Layout

After you've created your table, you can make changes to the layout if you need. You can resize the columns and rows by clicking and dragging the borders. Also, you can merge or split cells as you would in Excel.

To merge cells, select the rows or columns you would like to combine. Then on the Table menu, click Merge Cells, as shown in Figure 2-28.

To split cells, select the row or column you would like to divide. Click Table ➤ Split Cells. In the Split Cells dialog box, shown in Figure 2-29, specify the number of rows or columns you would like to create. After you've specified the options, click OK.

Figure 2-28. *Merging table cells*

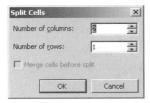

Figure 2-29. *The Split Cells dialog box*

Formatting Tables

If you didn't specify an AutoFormat when you created your table, or if you want to change the format you applied, you can still format your table.

To apply formatting to the characters in your table, select the text and use the buttons on the Formatting toolbar to change character attributes.

If you want to change text alignment or table alignment, or apply borders and shading, you'll need to use the Table Properties dialog box, as shown in Figure 2-30. You can access this by selecting a portion of your table, right-clicking, and selecting Table Properties.

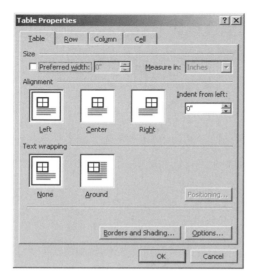

Figure 2-30. *The Table Properties dialog box*

To change text alignment, open the Cell tab, shown in Figure 2-31, and specify text alignment properties. You can choose Top, Center, or Bottom. If you want to change text wrapping within cells, click the Options button. Specify whether you want text to wrap to the next line or to fit on one line. Click OK.

Figure 2-31. *The Cell tab of the Table Properties dialog box*

To change the table alignment, open the Table tab in the Table Properties dialog box, as shown in Figure 2-32. Select how you want Word to align the table on the page. For more control, you can specify a left indentation for the table.

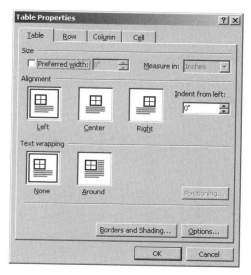

Figure 2-32. *The Table tab of the Table Properties dialog box*

You also have the option of wrapping document text around the table. For business plans, you should turn text wrapping off.

You can specify margins for text within the cell and padding between the cells. This allows you to space your data nicely across the page. To access these controls, as shown in Figure 2-33, click the Options button.

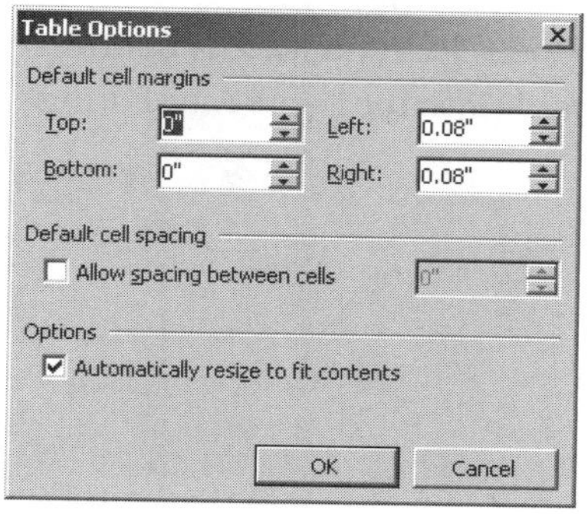

Figure 2-33. *Options for specifying cell margins and padding*

If you want to add borders or shading to cells, click the Borders and Shading button.

On the Borders tab, select the border style, color, and width. There are border presets that will apply the border style you choose to specific areas of the table. Or, you can click in the diagram on the right to specify where you want the borders to appear, as shown in Figure 2-34.

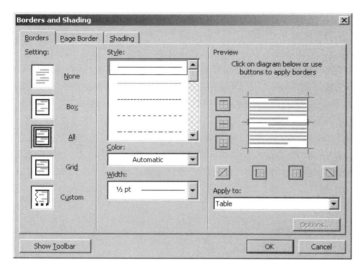

Figure 2-34. *Adding borders to a table*

To specify shading, open the Shading tab (see Figure 2-35). Select the color you would like to apply from the color chart. For more options, click More Colors. In the Patterns sections, you can select a shading pattern. Finally, click OK.

To change a table that you've AutoFormatted, click in the table. Click Table ➤ Table AutoFormat. In the Table AutoFormat dialog box, click Modify. In the Modify Style dialog box, enter a new name for the table style, as shown in Figure 2-36. Then use the controls to change the table formats. When you're done, click OK and close the Table AutoFormat dialog box.

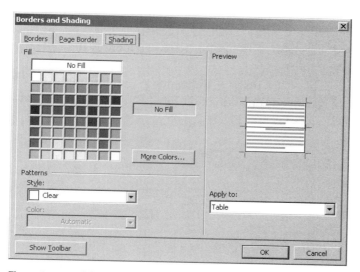

Figure 2-35. *Adding shading to table cells*

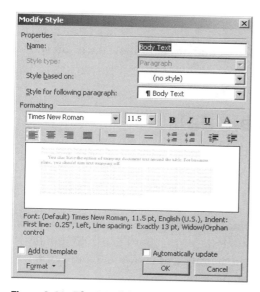

Figure 2-36. *The Modify Style dialog box*

Adding Captions to Your Tables

You may want to add a caption to your table. The caption helps you identify the table when you refer to it in your business plan.

To insert a caption, select your table. Click Insert ➤ Reference ➤ Caption. In the Label box, select the type of label. Then specify the position of the label. Enter the caption text in the box labeled Caption. Finally, click OK (see Figure 2-37).

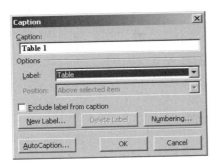

Figure 2-37. *The Caption dialog box*

Word inserts the caption as a field. The numbering updates automatically if you add more captions or rearrange captioned objects.

Generating Charts from Table Data

The easiest way to create a chart in your business plan is to use existing data that is contained within a table in your document.

To create a chart based on table data, select the chart by clicking inside it. Then click Table ➤ Select ➤ Table.

Once you have selected the entire table, click Insert ➤ Picture ➤ Chart. Word launches Microsoft Graph, which automatically creates a chart based on your table. Additionally, Word adds two new menus, Data and Chart, to the menubar, as shown in Figure 2-38. These menus will help you manipulate your chart.

The default chart type is a column chart. But you can change that. To do so, select your chart. Then click Chart ➤ Chart Type. The Chart Type dialog box provides you with a number of different chart styles, as you see in Figure 2-39. Simply select the type of chart you would like and click OK. Word returns you to your document and updates the chart automatically.

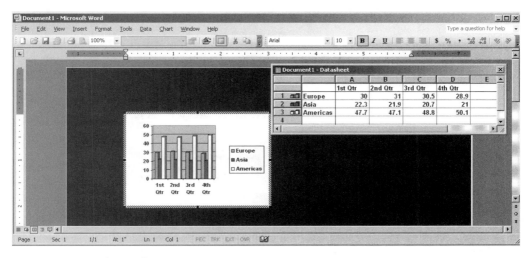

Figure 2-38. *Inserting a chart*

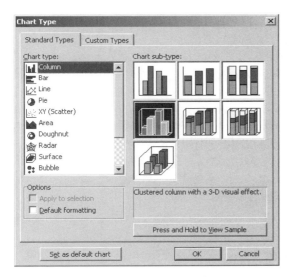

Figure 2-39. *The Chart Type dialog box*

When you create a chart, Word automatically opens a data sheet where you can modify the information represented in the chart. The first column of the data sheet contains the data series. These are the items that are plotted on the graph. The first row of the data sheet contains the categories. The categories appear along the horizontal axis of the chart. The cells where the rows and columns intersect contain the values.

You can change the way your chart represents the data. Simply choose Data and select Series in Columns or Series in Rows.

Specifying Chart Options

A good chart will have a clear title, a legend, and labels. You can specify these elements by selecting your chart and then clicking Chart ➤ Chart Options. Available options will vary, depending on the type of chart.

On the Titles tab, shown in Figure 2-40, you can specify a title for the entire chart and titles for the axes. Changes appear immediately in the preview section.

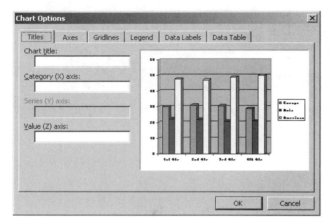

Figure 2-40. *The Titles tab of the Chart Options dialog box*

On the Axes tab, you can change the labels that appear along each axis (see Figure 2-41). This can prove handy if space is limited. However, be careful not to sacrifice the chart's clarity.

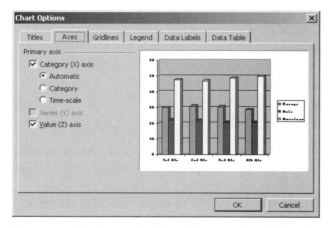

Figure 2-41. *The Axes tab of the Chart Options dialog box*

On the Gridlines tab, shown in Figure 2-42, you can specify what gridlines you want to add to the chart, which can make it easier to read a chart.

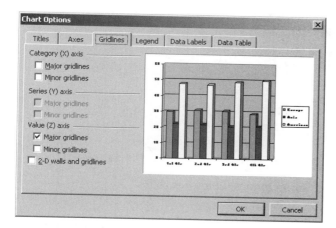

Figure 2-42. *The Gridlines tab of the Chart Options dialog box*

Word automatically inserts a legend in your chart. The Legend tab, shown in Figure 2-43, allows you to change the position of the legend. You can also opt to remove the legend from the chart.

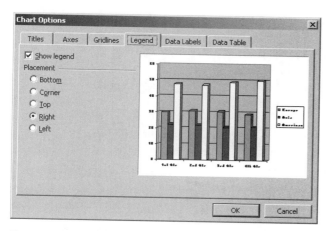

Figure 2-43. *The Legend tab of the Chart Options dialog box*

The Data Labels tab lets you add additional labels to your chart (see Figure 2-44). These labels can bring more clarity to the chart. However, they can also make the chart seem cluttered.

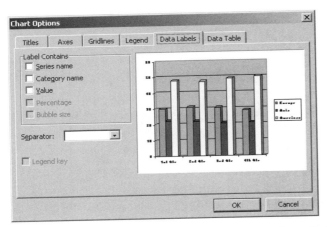

Figure 2-44. *The Data Labels tab of the Chart Options dialog box*

The Data Table tab, shown in Figure 2-45, lets you include the table upon which the chart is based in the chart. You may want to use this feature if the data table is on a different page, or if it isn't clear that the table is related to the chart.

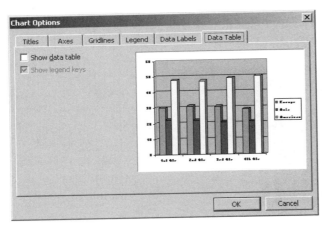

Figure 2-45. *The Data Table tab of the Chart Options dialog box*

Finally, you have the option of changing the formatting of specific elements of the chart. Simply right-click an element within the chart. Word presents you with appropriate formatting options. The options will vary widely, depending on the type of chart and the chart element you selected.

Adding Captions to Charts

As with tables, you may want to add a caption to your chart. The caption helps you identify the table when you refer to it in your business plan.

To insert a caption, select the chart. Click Insert ➤ Reference ➤ Caption. In the Label box, select the type of label, as shown in Figure 2-46. Then specify the position of the label. Enter the caption text in the box labeled Caption. Finally, click OK.

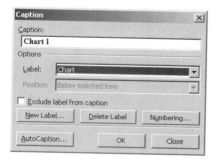

Figure 2-46. *The Caption dialog box*

Word inserts the caption as a field. The numbering updates automatically if you add more captions or rearrange captioned objects.

Working with Headers and Footers

You should add a header and/or footer to your business plan. While you can use these sections to list important information, use them sparingly.

You should include page numbers in the footer to ensure that the business plan can be reordered easily should someone separate the pages. You should not number the cover page. However, if the table of contents runs over one page, you may want to number it.

To number the table of contents, place your cursor at the top of the first page. Click View ➤ Header and Footer. Click the Page Setup button on the Header and Footer toolbar. Use the controls to specify the distance from the edge of the paper (see Figure 2-47). In the Preview section, select This point forward. Click OK.

Scroll down and click within the footer box. On the Formatting toolbar, click the Right Alignment button. Then on the Header and Footer toolbar, click the Insert Page Number button. Click the Format Page Number button. In the Page Number Format dialog box, shown in Figure 2-48, select the number format. For a table of contents, use lowercase Roman numerals. Under Page numbering, select Start at and use the controls to select "i." Click OK.

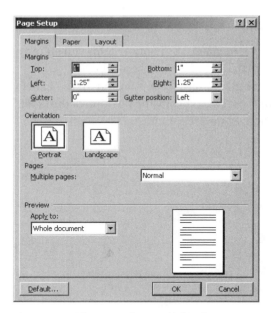

Figure 2-47. *The Page Setup dialog box*

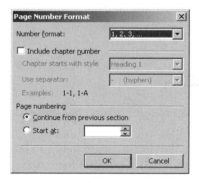

Figure 2-48. *The Page Number Format dialog box*

To add page number to the remainder of the business plan, place your cursor at the top of the first page. Click View ➤ Header and Footer. Click the Page Setup button on the Header and Footer toolbar. Use the controls to specify the distance from the edge of the paper. In the Preview section, select This point forward. Click OK.

Scroll down and click within the footer box. On the Formatting toolbar, click the Right Alignment button. Then on the Header and Footer toolbar, click the Insert Page Number button. Click the Format Page Number button. In the Page Number Format box, select the number format. You should select standard numbering. Under Page numbering, select Start at and use the controls to select the appropriate page number. Click OK.

The process for adding headers is the same as for footers.

CHAPTER 3

Creating Marketing Brochures and Newsletters

At first glance, marketing brochures and newsletters seem like very different types of documents. However, both include identical elements, such as pictures, columns, and borders. The steps for formatting brochures and newsletters are similar, even though the results will look very different.

With brochures and newsletters, you should start by creating a basic document. Add as much of the document text and as many of the formatting styles as you can. However, formatting a brochure or newsletter will require much more advanced features. You may find that you need to go back and tweak some of your earlier work. This is to be expected with intricately formatted documents.

You'll find a sample marketing brochure with the downloads for this book at the Apress web site (http://www.apress.com).

Specifying Page Setup

After entering the body text, you are ready to specify the page setup for the entire document. You may decide later to alter the page setup in specific parts of your newsletter or brochure. Or you may already know that the page setup will differ in certain areas. This is okay. For now, you are setting the predominant page layout for your document.

Access the Page Setup dialog box by clicking File ➤ Page Setup. Click the Margins tab to open the settings for the margins, as shown in Figure 3-1.

The default settings for the Normal.dot template are 1 inch at the top and bottom of the page and 1.25 inches at either side of the page. You can enter new margin sizes if you wish.

You may also want to change the page orientation. In most documents, the vertical edge of the page is longer than the horizontal edge. This is *portrait orientation*. But in some situations, you want the horizontal edge to be longer. This is called *landscape orientation*.

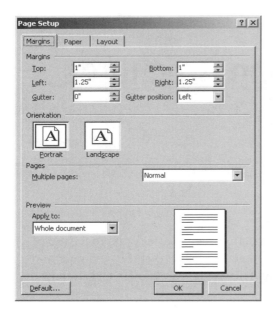

Figure 3-1. *The Margins tab of the Page Setup dialog box*

In the Orientation section, select Portrait or Landscape by clicking the appropriate button.

If you want the document from the cursor position forward to change to Landscape orientation, you must specify it. In the Preview section, select This point forward in the drop-down box. Otherwise the change will apply to the entire document.

■**Tip** You can apply Landscape orientation to one or more pages in the middle of your document. The easiest way to do this is to select a portion of your document. Then follow the preceding steps. In the Preview section, choose Selected text from the drop-down box. Also, if you have created sections in your document, you can click in a section, follow the preceding steps, but select This section in the Preview section.

Next, click the Paper tab in the Page Setup dialog box to display the options shown in Figure 3-2. In the Paper size section, use the drop-down box to specify the paper size.

Use the boxes in the Paper source section to specify the printer's paper tray(s) for the first page of the newsletter or brochure and for the subsequent pages. In the Preview section, opt to apply the changes to the whole document.

Click the Print Options button to review the settings, as you see in Figure 3-3. Deselect Draft output if it has been selected. You should select Drawing objects.

Once you have made your selections, click OK.

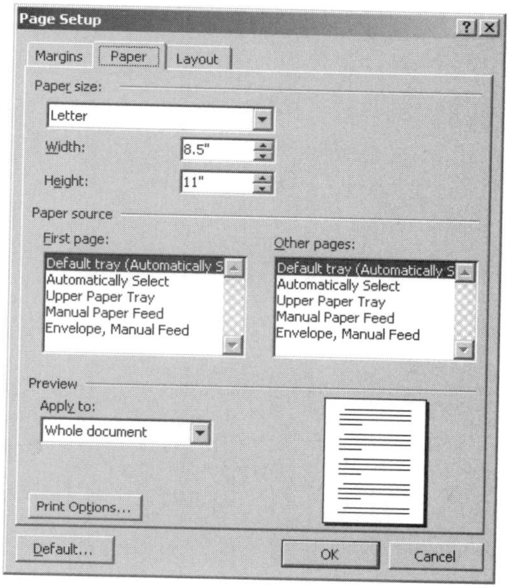

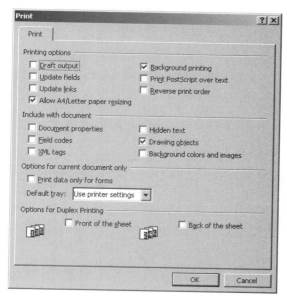

Figure 3-2. *The Paper tab of the Page Setup dialog box*

Figure 3-3. *The Print dialog box*

On the Layout tab, as shown in Figure 3-4, check the document's vertical alignment. Select the alignment in the drop-down box. Opt to apply the changes to the whole document or that point forward. Click OK.

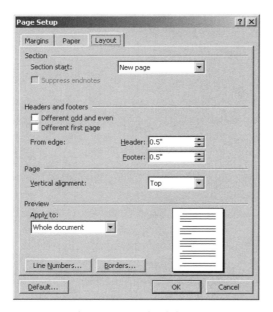

Figure 3-4. *The Layout tab of the Page Setup dialog box*

TAKING ADVANTAGE OF WORD'S SECTIONS FEATURE

When you're working in Word, you will find it advantageous to divide your document into sections.
You can insert a section break by clicking Insert ➤ Break. In the Break dialog box, you have a number of options in the section labeled Section break types. They are as follows:

- *Next page*: This inserts a section break in the document. Text following the break will begin on a new page.

- *Continuous*: Word inserts a section break at the cursor position. Text following the break does not move. It remains on the current page.

- *Even page*: Word inserts a section break in the document. Text following the break will move to the subsequent even page.

- *Odd page*: This inserts a section break at the cursor position. Text following the break will move to the next odd page.

In printed documents, one section is not distinguishable from the next. However, by dividing your document into sections, you are simplifying the formatting process. Word often gives you the option of applying page formatting at the section level. You determine what constitutes a section of the document.

Inserting Columns in Your Newsletter or Brochure

Columns can give your document a clean, refined look. Also, text is easier to read when you break it up into shorter lines. Columns can be tricky if you don't use them correctly. But when you understand a few key points, they're relatively simple.

The easiest way to apply columns to a portion of your document is to use the Columns button on the Standard toolbar. Select a portion of your document and click the button. A drop-down menu gives you the option of dividing the section into four columns, as you see in Figure 3-5. However, if you hold the left mouse button and drag to the right, you are given the option of adding six columns. Simply highlight the number of columns you want to apply.

Figure 3-5. *Creating columns using the Columns toolbar button*

■**Tip** Columns provide an easy way to create trifold brochures. Set your document orientation to Landscape in the Page Setup dialog box. Then divide the entire document into three columns.

This doesn't give you many choices. For more advanced options, click Format ➤ Columns.

You can select from the Presets column designs, as shown in Figure 3-6. Or, you can specify the number of columns you want by using the Number of columns box. Word supports up to 12 columns in Portrait orientation and 18 columns in Landscape orientation.

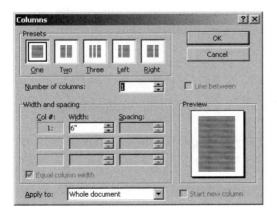

Figure 3-6. *The Columns dialog box*

By default, Word makes each column identical in width. But you can set the width for each column independently. Deselect Equal column width. Then use the controls to specify width, in inches, for each column. The Spacing boxes let you set the distance between the columns.

If you would like a line between each column, select Line between. Use the Preview section to see how your columns will look.

Tip For greater control over the appearance of columns, you can insert column breaks. This will push all text after the break into the next column. So you won't need to enter returns to move text. To insert a column break, click Insert ➤ Break. Select Column break and click OK.

Finally, choose Selected text in the Apply to drop-down box. Or, you can select Whole document to apply it to the entire document. If text isn't selected, your choices are This point forward or Whole document. Click OK.

Caution Columns can become problematic in some situations. That's because Word must create a new section when you change the number of columns in your document. So keep this in mind if you're working with other elements that change from section to section.

Applying Borders and Shading

You can spice up the appearance of your document by adding borders and shading to portions of it. The colors and lines will add graphical impact.

As with any type of creative formatting, use borders and shading sparingly. Otherwise, the elements will overwhelm the document and distract your readers. Additionally, when you're creating a document for a professional audience, avoid ornate or overly whimsical border types.

Adding Shading

To add shading, select the portion of your document you would like to highlight with a color. Then click Format ➤ Borders and Shading.

On the Shading tab, shown in Figure 3-7, use the color grid to select a fill color. You can click the More Colors button if you would like a wider range of colors, or if you would like to create a custom color.

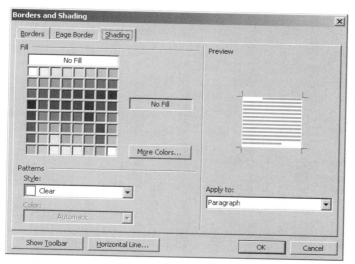

Figure 3-7. *The Shading tab of the Borders and Shading dialog box*

Word also allows you to apply a pattern to the shaded area. Use the Style drop-down box in the Patterns area to select a pattern. You can also select the alternating color for the pattern. Simply use the drop-down box labeled Color to select one.

Word will apply shading in one of two ways. First, you can opt to apply the shading at the text level by select Text in the Preview section. This does not apply the shading to spaces at the end of lines or to spacing between lines. If a paragraph is double-spaced, for example, there will be gaps between the lines of text. Plus, the ends of lines will look jagged.

For a cleaner look, apply the shading at the paragraph level by selecting Paragraph in the Preview section. The shading will extend from margin to margin in the selected area. Furthermore, you don't need to worry about gaps between lines of text.

Once you have applied your shading, click OK.

Applying a Border to a Portion of Your Brochure or Newsletter

Applying a border to a portion of your document is similar to applying shading. Select the portion of your document you would like to highlight with a border. Then click Format ➤ Borders and Shading.

On the Borders tab, select a line style in the Style section, shown in Figure 3-8. Simply scroll through the options and select one of the line styles.

Next, use the Color drop-down box to specify the border line color. Click the More Line Colors button at the bottom of the list for a greater range of options. This also allows you to create a custom color to use.

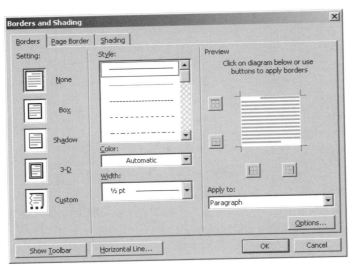

Figure 3-8. *The Borders tab of the Borders and Shading dialog box*

After you've selected a color, select a line weight in the Width drop-down box. Finally, click in the Preview area to apply the border to specific sides of the selected text or paragraph. Or, you can select from a preset in the Setting section.

■Tip You're not required to use the same border on all sides of selected text or paragraphs. For varying borders, select a border style and apply it to one portion of the text in the Preview area. Then select a second border style and apply it to another. You can repeat this for the remaining two borders. By using this ability wisely, you can create borders that look three-dimensional.

To specify the distance between the text and border, click the Options button. In the Borders and Shading Options dialog box, shown in Figure 3-9, you have a number of options for border spacing.

Word will apply borders in one of two ways. First, you can opt to apply the shading at the text level by selecting Text in the Preview section. This does not apply the border to spaces at the end of lines. Also, you will see the border between lines of text.

For a cleaner look, apply the border at the paragraph level by selecting Paragraph in the Preview section. The border will enclose the entire selected area with one clean rectangle.

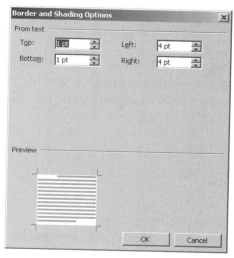

Figure 3-9. *The Borders and Shading Options dialog box*

Adding a Border to an Entire Page

You can also place a border around the entire page or multiple pages. This is handy if the text on a page may change. You can add or remove text without affecting the border of the page.

To add a page border, click Format ➤ Borders and Shading. Open the Page Border tab, the options of which are shown in Figure 3-10. Specifying options for a page border is similar to specifying options for a border around text or a paragraph. There are two exceptions.

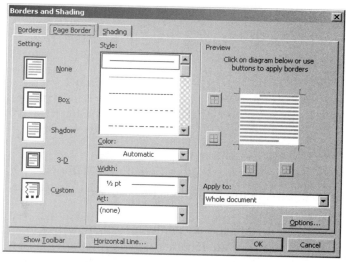

Figure 3-10. *The Page Border tab of the Borders and Shading dialog box*

You can add decorative borders by clicking the Art drop-down box. Decorative borders are only available if they were installed with Word. Furthermore, they are generally not appropriate for professional documents.

You can also specify which pages will have the border. In the Preview section, you have a number of choices in the Apply to drop-down box. But, to take advantage of most of them, you must use section breaks in your document. For information on section breaks, see the sidebar "Taking Advantage of Word's Sections Feature" earlier in this chapter.

Once you have specified your options, click OK.

Inserting Pictures

Images are an important part of marketing brochures and newsletters. You can insert photographs and other images into a Word document in a few simple steps. And Word provides you with a number of options for formatting them perfectly.

To insert an image, click Insert ➤ Picture ➤ From File to bring up the Insert Picture dialog box shown in Figure 3-11. Navigate through this dialog box to find the correct image. Word accepts a wide variety of image types.

Figure 3-11. *The Insert Picture dialog box*

When you find your image, select it and click Insert. The image will appear at the current cursor position.

It is also possible to insert a picture by copying it from a different program, such as a photo editing program. Then select the place in your document where you want to insert the image and use the Ctrl+V keyboard shortcut to paste the picture into the document.

Editing Pictures

When you click an image in Word, the Picture toolbar appears, as shown in Figure 3-12. It provides a number of options for editing your picture, such as adjusting brightness, contrast, and color. You can also crop images or rotate them.

Figure 3-12. *The Picture toolbar*

■**Caution** Word provides you with a number of options for editing pictures you insert in your document. I strongly advise that you avoid editing your images in Word. Rather, you should use a program that is designed specifically for editing images and edit the images before inserting them in the document for two reasons. First, you'll get better images. Second, you won't end up with a bloated file.

To crop a picture, click the Crop button. A black bar appears on each side of the picture, plus on each corner. Click and drag the bars to move the edge of the picture. When you've made your adjustments, click outside of the picture.

The Text Wrapping button helps you position the picture in relation to the text. Click the button and select an option from the drop-down menu that appears, as shown in Figure 3-13.

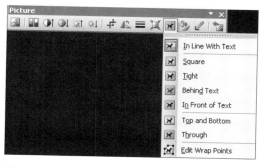

Figure 3-13. *Picture text wrapping options*

To align your picture in relation to the document margins, select it and then click one of the alignment buttons on the Formatting toolbar.

You can resize the picture by clicking and dragging the black boxes on the edges and or in the corners of the picture.

For more advanced formatting options, right-click your picture and select Format Picture to open the Format Picture dialog box.

The Size tab of this dialog box, shown in Figure 3-14, lets you manually set the size of your picture. You can also scale your picture by percentage. To keep the picture proportions, select Lock aspect ratio.

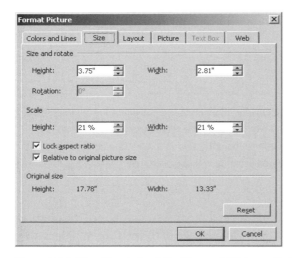

Figure 3-14. *The Size tab of the Format Picture dialog box*

On the Layout tab, shown in Figure 3-15, you can specify text wrapping and horizontal alignment.

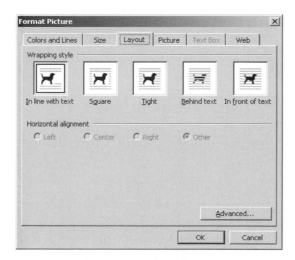

Figure 3-15. *The Layout tab of the Format Picture dialog box*

The Advanced button opens the Advanced Layout dialog box, as shown in Figure 3-16. On the Text Wrapping tab, you can specify the distance between the picture and text. You can also specify text wrapping for specific sides of the picture.

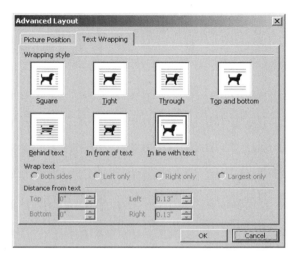

Figure 3-16. *The Text Wrapping tab of the Advanced Layout dialog box*

On the Picture Position tab, shown in Figure 3-17, select both vertical and horizontal alignment options. You can also set the alignment in relation to specific elements of the document. Once you've made your changes, click OK to return to the Format Picture dialog box.

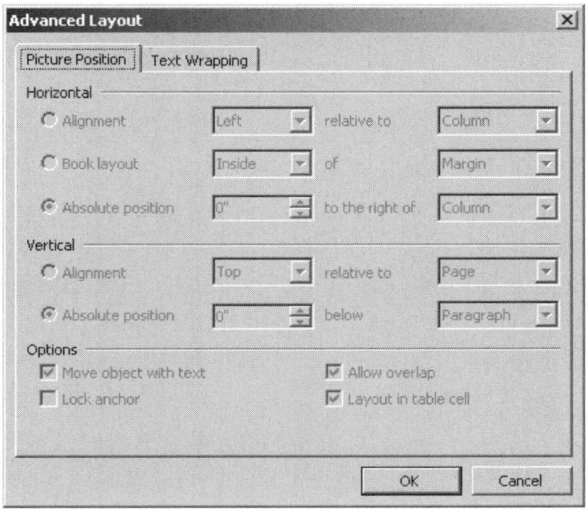

Figure 3-17. *The Picture Position Tab of the Advanced Layout Dialog Box*

On the Picture tab, shown in Figure 3-18, you can specify picture cropping in inches. You can also make changes to the image brightness and contrast.

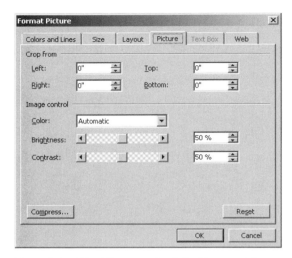

Figure 3-18. *The Picture tab of the Format Picture dialog box*

Inserting WordArt

WordArt can be an effective way to call attention to text in a brochure or newsletter. WordArt is text that is formatted to look like a picture. Exercise caution when using this feature. If you use it too frequently, it loses effectiveness and overwhelms the reader. And, if you use it incorrectly, it will make your document appear amateurish.

To insert WordArt, position your cursor where you want it to appear in your document. Then click Insert ➤ Picture ➤ WordArt. In the WordArt Gallery, shown in Figure 3-19, select a style and click OK.

In the Edit WordArt Text dialog box, shown in Figure 3-20, specify the font, font size, and bold and/or italics. Then type the word or phrase and click OK.

Word gives you a wide variety of options for formatting WordArt. When you click the WordArt, the WordArt toolbar appears.

You can edit the text by clicking the Edit Text button. The WordArt Gallery button lets you specify a different style for the WordArt, or you can click the WordArt Shape button to fit the WordArt to a different shape.

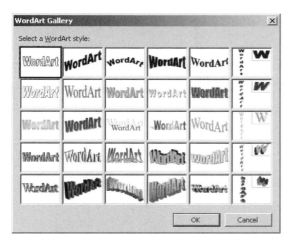

Figure 3-19. *The WordArt Gallery*

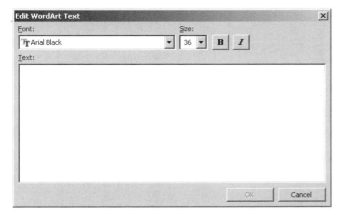

Figure 3-20. *The Edit WordArt Text dialog box*

To specify the WordArt's position in relation to the document text, click the Text Wrapping button and select a position from the drop-down list, as you see in Figure 3-21.

To make all letters the same height, click the WordArt Same Letter Heights button. This button, like the WordArt Vertical Text button, works as a toggle.

You can use the WordArt Alignment button to specify the alignment. Additionally, the WordArt Character Spacing button provides a menu to set the distance between letter and character kerning.

For more advanced options, click the Format WordArt button. It opens the Format WordArt dialog box, which offers a bevy of options.

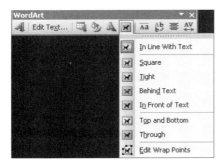

Figure 3-21. *WordArt text wrapping options*

On the Colors and Lines tab, shown in Figure 3-22, you can set the word border colors, style, and weight. To change the fill color, click the Color drop-down box and pick a color from the chart. For more color choices, click Custom Color. The Fill Effects button at the bottom of the color menu opens the Fill Effects dialog box. There you can specify gradients, textures, pattern, and even pictures. Click OK to return to the Format WordArt dialog box.

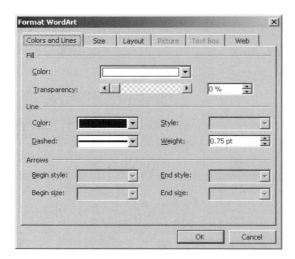

Figure 3-22. *The Colors and Lines tab of the Format WordArt dialog box*

On the Size tab, which you can see in Figure 3-23, specify height and width in inches or use the scale options to set a percentage. You can also rotate the WordArt.

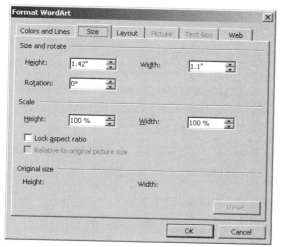

Figure 3-23. *The Size tab of the Format WordArt dialog box*

The Layout tab of the Format WordArt dialog box, shown in Figure 3-24, functions the same as the Layout tab in the Format Picture dialog box.

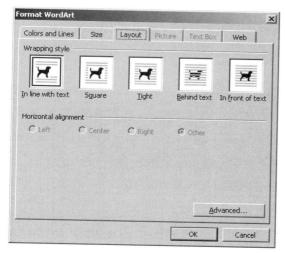

Figure 3-24. *The Layout tab of the Format WordArt dialog box*

Once you've made your choices, click OK to view the WordArt.

Working with Text Boxes

If you want greater control over the position of a block of text in your document, consider using text boxes. You can place these boxes anywhere in the document and format them with shading and borders.

Additionally, you can link text boxes so that the contents flow between the boxes automatically. This is convenient if you want to insert a story that begins on one page of a newsletter and continues on a different page.

To insert a text box, click Insert ➤ Text Box. Click and drag your mouse where you would like to position the box in your document. It will appear with a border that you can use to resize or reposition the text box, as Figure 3-25 demonstrates.

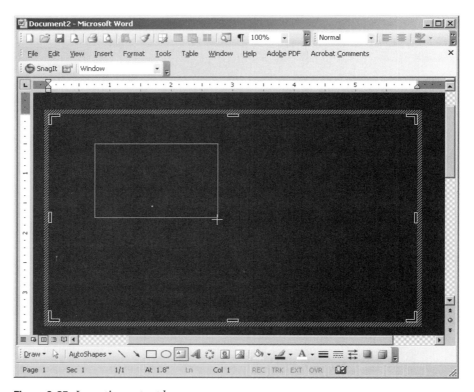

Figure 3-25. *Inserting a text box*

■Note By default, Word places text boxes in a drawing canvas. You may find this inconvenient. You can drag the text box off the canvas. Then you can delete the canvas by selecting it and pressing Delete. You can also disable the drawing canvas by clicking Tools ➤ Options and opening the General tab. Deselect Automatically Create Drawing Canvas When Inserting AutoShapes and click OK.

You can enter text in the box simply by clicking and typing in the box. You can format the text in the box as you would other text in your document. This includes character and paragraph formatting, as well as the use of styles. You can't use some formatting, such as columns, page breaks, and drop caps. Additionally, text boxes cannot contain tables of contents, comments, or footnotes.

■Tip If the text you want to insert in a text box requires heavy formatting, enter it in a separate document. Format the text as you would like it to appear in the newsletter or brochure. Then cut and paste it into the text box. This is often easier than working directly in the text box.

By default, text boxes are white with a thin black border. To change the background color, click the Fill button on the Drawing toolbar. Select a color from the color chart, shown in Figure 3-26, or use the More Fill Colors button at the bottom for more choices, including custom colors. You can use the Fill Effects button to specify background patterns.

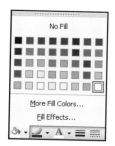

Figure 3-26. *Using the Fill button on the Drawing toolbar*

To change the border, click the Line button on the Drawing toolbar. Select a color from the chart, shown in Figure 3-27, or click More Line Colors for more choices, including custom colors. The Patterned Lines button lets you change the border style.

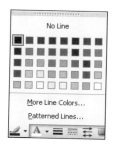

Figure 3-27. *Using the Line button on the Drawing toolbar*

■**Note** The default background color for text boxes is white. It is not transparent. To remove the background color altogether, click the Fill button on the Drawing toolbar. Then select No Fill from the pop-up menu.

For more advanced formatting options, right-click the border of a text box and select Format Text Box.

On the Colors and Lines tab of this dialog box, shown in Figure 3-28, you can change the background color and adjust the transparency. You can also specify border style, color, and weight.

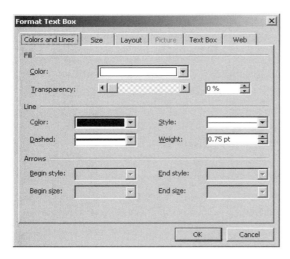

Figure 3-28. *The Colors and Lines tab of the Format Text Box dialog box*

The Size tab lets you specify dimensions in inches or scale the text box size by entering percentages, as you can see in Figure 3-29.

The Text Box tab, shown in Figure 3-30, lets you specify internal margins. You can also turn word wrapping on or off and specify that the box automatically resize to fit the text.

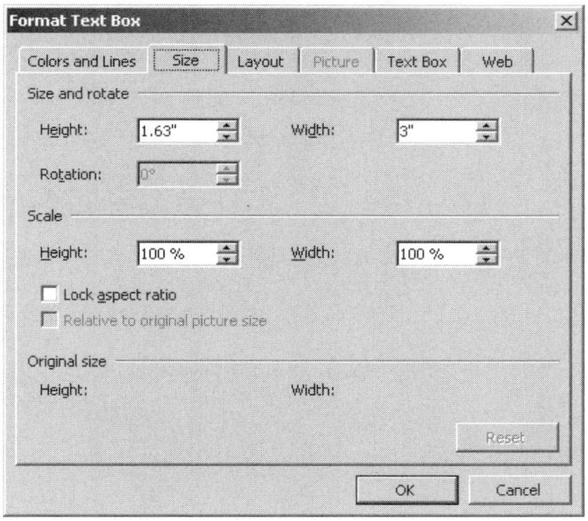

Figure 3-29. *The Size tab of the Format Text Box dialog box*

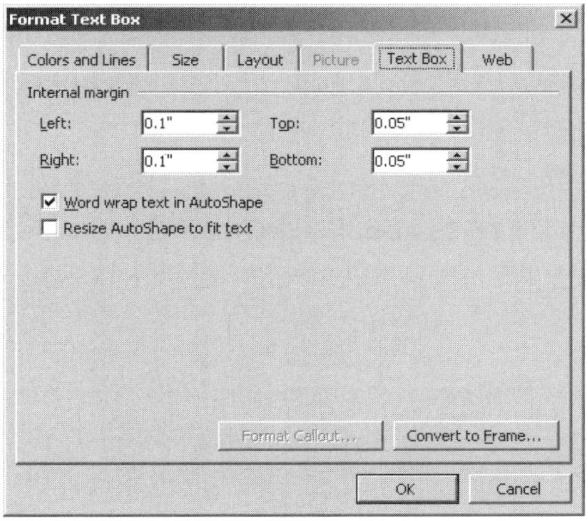

Figure 3-30. *The Text Box tab of the Format Text Box dialog box*

As you can see in Figure 3-31, the Layout tab of the Format Text Box dialog box offers the same options as the Layout tab in the Format Picture dialog box.

Once you've specified your options, click OK.

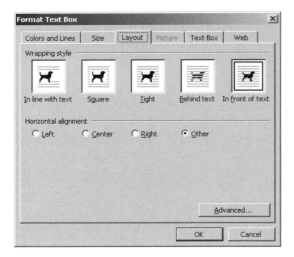

Figure 3-31. *The Layout tab of the Format Text Box dialog box*

Linking Text Boxes

You can link text boxes so that text flows automatically from one box to the next. This is handy for portions of your document that start on one page and continue on one or more subsequent pages.

First, create your text boxes in Print Layout view (click View ➤ Print Layout). Do not enter any text until you've linked the boxes. Click the first box; the Text Box toolbar opens, as shown in Figure 3-32. Click the Create Text Box Link button and then click the second text box.

Figure 3-32. *The Text Box toolbar*

If you wish to link additional boxes, you can do so by clicking the Create Text Box Link button. The links function as a chain. This means each box must be linked to the box before it, not to the first text box.

Once you've created your links, enter the text in the first box. Word automatically flows the text between the boxes. As you edit it, the text automatically reflows.

You can use the Next Text Box and Previous Text Box buttons to move between the linked boxes.

It can prove tricky to remove a box from the middle of a linked chain of boxes. To remove a box without breaking the flow, right-click its border and select Cut. The box is removed, and the text reflows.

If you wish to break the link between a box and the one that follows, click the box. Then click the Break Forward Link button on the Text Box toolbar. This essentially creates two series of linked text boxes. The first series contains the text; the second series will be empty.

Adding Captions to Tables, Charts, and Pictures

You may want to add a caption to your table, picture, or chart. The caption helps you identify these objects when you refer to them in your document.

To insert a caption, select your table. Click Insert ➤ Reference ➤ Caption. In the Label box, select the type of label. Then specify the position of the label. Enter the caption text in the box labeled Caption, as shown in Figure 3-33. Finally, click OK.

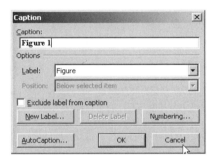

Figure 3-33. *The Caption dialog box*

Word inserts the caption as a field. The numbering updates automatically if you add more captions or rearrange captioned objects.

Specifying Print Options

When you're working on brochures and newsletters, you may want to print on both sides of the paper. Word provides features that will help you with duplex printing.

If your printer does not have an automatic duplex feature, you can do it manually. Open the Print dialog box, shown in Figure 3-34, by clicking File ➤ Print. In the Print drop-down box, select Odd pages and then click OK to start printing.

Once the odd pages have printed, put the pages back in your printer. Open the Print dialog box again and select Even pages in the Print drop-down box. You may have to experiment with your printer to get it right.

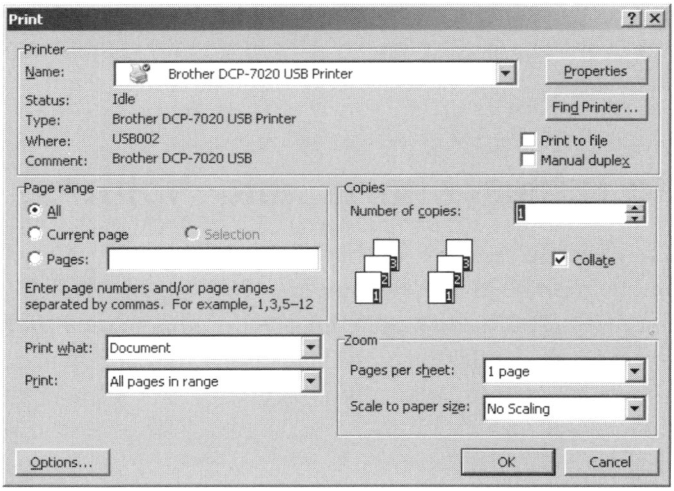

Figure 3-34. *The Print dialog box*

If you have a printer that does automatic duplex printing, open the Print dialog box. Click the Options button. In the Options for Duplex Printing section, shown in Figure 3-35, specify your printing options. Click OK. Then click OK in the Print dialog box to begin printing.

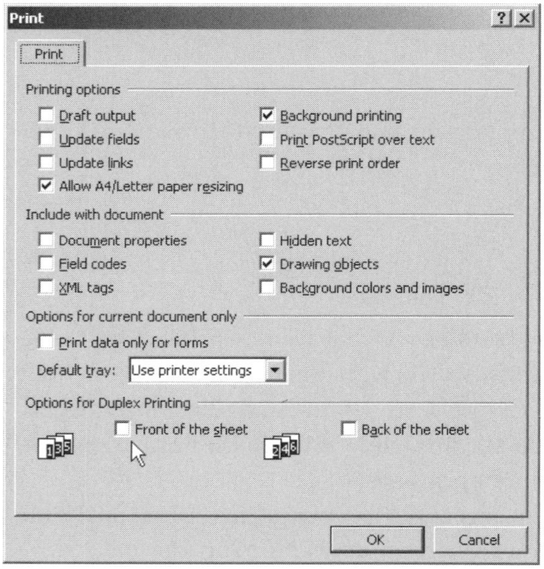

Figure 3-35. *Specifying duplex printing options*

Scaling Your Brochure or Document to a Different Paper Size

When you create a document, you create it for a specific paper size. Changing the document's paper size after the document has been created will wreak havoc on the formatting.

Word does, however, provide an easy way for you to print your document on a different paper size without changing the formatting. The Scaling option allows you to preserve the formatting of the original document. It simply resizes everything to a new paper size.

To scale your document, click File ➤ Print. In the Print dialog box, select your new paper size in the box labeled Scale to paper size. It is in the Zoom section. Click OK to begin printing.

■■■

Creating Forms for Printing or Distributing Electronically

With Word, you can create forms that are printed and completed by hand. Or, you can create forms that can be completed electronically. While their preparation is relatively similar, they serve differing purposes. Electronic forms are easier to manage and give the creator greater control over their contents.

For a sample form, visit the downloads section for this book at the Apress web site (http://www.apress.com).

Designing a Form

When you create a form, Word's Outline view probably isn't the best way to plan the document. Rather, it makes more sense to draw the layout of the form on a piece of paper. This will help you decide what form elements to use and where to position them on the page.

A printed form that you create in Word can have several different elements. You can add text form fields, check box form fields, and floating frames. Additionally, you may want to use a table to arrange the various form sections on the page.

If you decide to use a table to organize your form, creating the table should be your first step.

Open the Forms toolbar by right-clicking in the toolbar area. Select Forms from the pop-up list, as shown in Figure 4-1.

The easiest way to create a table for forms is to draw it using your mouse. Click the Draw Table button to begin drawing your table. The Tables and Borders toolbar opens (see Figure 4-2).

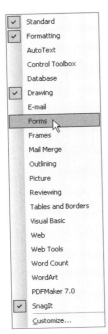

Figure 4-1. *Selecting the Forms toolbar*

Figure 4-2. *The Tables and Borders toolbar*

Before you begin drawing, use the drop-down boxes to select the table's line style and line weight. You can also use the Border Color button to select a different color for the table lines. Then create your layout table by clicking where you want the top-left corner to begin. Drag your mouse and release the button where you want the bottom-right corner of the first cell to end, as Figure 4-3 demonstrates.

Repeat the steps for each cell of the table. Cells can vary in width and height. If you make a mistake while you're drawing the table, you can use the Eraser button to erase cells from the table by drawing a box around the cells to be deleted. Then click the Draw Table button to continue adding cells.

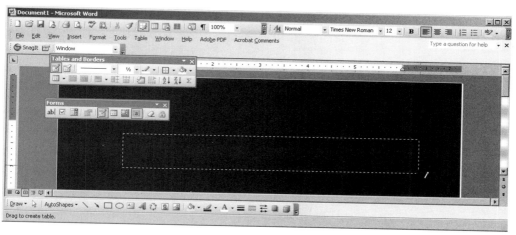

Figure 4-3. *Drawing a table cell*

If you don't want to draw the individual rows and columns of a table, you can use the Insert Table button. This will open a dialog box that allows you to specify the number of rows and columns for the table, as shown in Figure 4-4. They will be uniform in size.

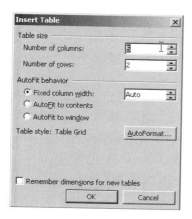

Figure 4-4. *Using the Insert Table button*

Additionally, you can split the cells in a table row. Click the Split Cells button on the toolbar. Then specify the desired number of rows and columns, and click OK. As Figure 4-5 illustrates, you can click and drag the cell borders to resize the cells.

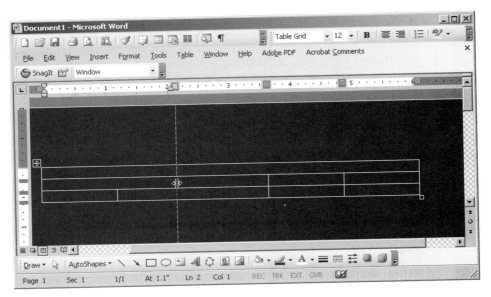

Figure 4-5. *Using the split cells feature*

If you need, you can also merge cells. Highlight the cells you would like to merge and click the Merge Cells button, as you see in Figure 4-6.

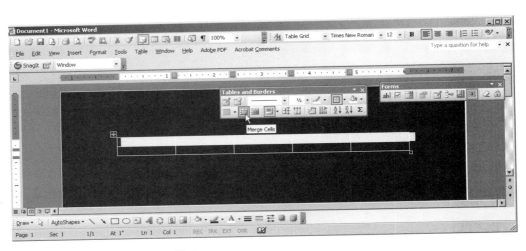

Figure 4-6. *Using the Merge Cells feature*

There are also buttons that will distribute the columns and rows evenly. Highlight the multiple columns or rows and then click the appropriate button, as shown in Figure 4-7. Word will resize them all to the same size.

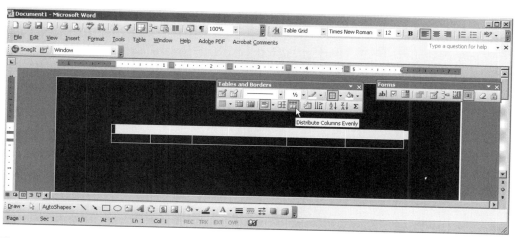

Figure 4-7. *The Distribute Columns Evenly button*

You can use the Fill button to apply shading to different cells in the table. This is handy for highlighting sections that are designed for office use only, for example. Just click the button to apply color to the cell where the mouse is currently positioned. Or select multiple cells and click the Fill button. You can use the arrow beside the button and select a different color from the pop-up color chart, if you desire (see Figure 4-8).

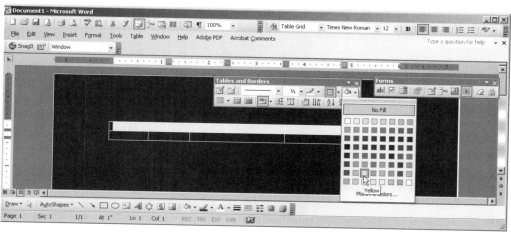

Figure 4-8. *Choosing fill options*

Entering Form Text and Form Fields

Next, you are ready to begin entering text and the form fields. Just click inside the cells and begin typing to enter the text. You can also insert pictures in the table cells. When you're ready to insert a form field, just select it from the Forms toolbar. It will appear inline with text.

To align the text in a table cell, click the Alignment button. The arrow to the right of it will give you a pop-up menu of options, as Figure 4-9 shows. Select the one you want for the cell contents.

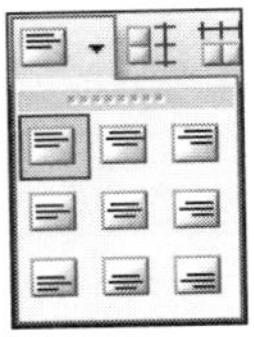

Figure 4-9. *Text alignment options*

If needed, you can change the direction of text within a cell. Simply click the Change Text Direction button, as shown in Figure 4-10.

Figure 4-10. *The Change Text Direction button*

With printed forms, there are only two important form fields to enter. The first is a text form field, which is a box where text can be entered. You can join several in succession if you need to resize the box, as shown in Figure 4-11.

The second form field is the check box form field, which is a box that users can simply check (see Figure 4-12).

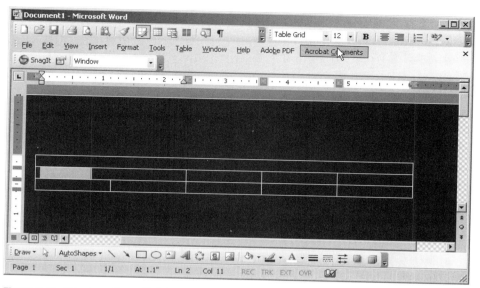

Figure 4-11. *The text form field*

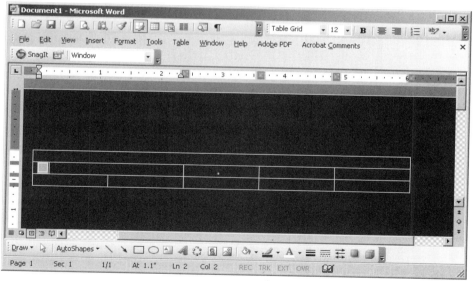

Figure 4-12. *The check box form field*

Additionally, the toolbar allows you to insert a frame in the document. This is handy if you want to include a small form in only a portion of your document, as shown in Figure 4-13.

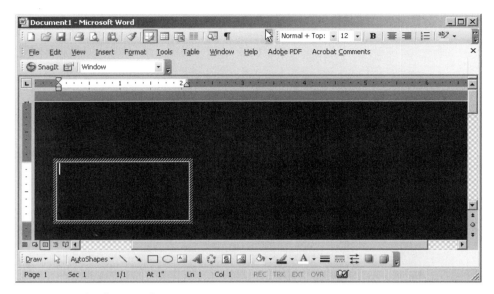

Figure 4-13. *The floating frame*

■**Tip** While working with form fields, it is helpful to turn on form field shading. Certain form fields are not visible with the shading turned off. The shading does not appear when you print the form. Additionally, you probably don't want to see field codes in your document; your fields will appear as a string of characters. To disable field codes, click Tools ➤ Options. On the View tab, uncheck Field Codes.

Once you have completed your form, you may wish to lock it. Simply click the Protect Form button on the Forms toolbar, shown in Figure 4-14, to prevent changes to the form layout and the text labels in the form.

Figure 4-14. *The Protect Form button*

Creating Forms for Electronic Distribution

Word also allows you to create forms that can be completed in Word. Such forms are similar to forms that are printed and then completed. However, you have more options.

First, you can insert a drop-down form field. This is similar to a form field that a user completes. However, the options are limited. The user clicks an arrow in the form field box and selects from a number of options.

To insert a drop-down form field, position the cursor where you would like the field to appear. Then click the Drop-Down Form Field button. The field will look similar to a regular form field, as you can see in Figure 4-15.

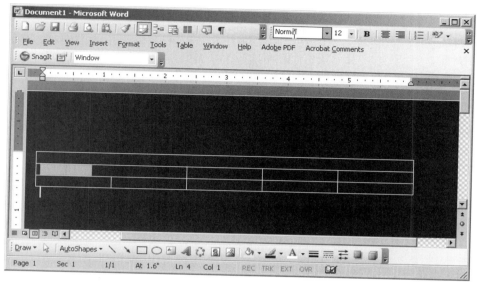

Figure 4-15. *The drop-down form field*

To specify options for the drop-down form field, right-click it and select Properties. The Drop-Down Form Field Options dialog box, shown in Figure 4-16, will open. Begin by entering items in the box labeled Drop-down item. After you have entered an item, click the Add button. It will appear in the box labeled Items in drop-down list.

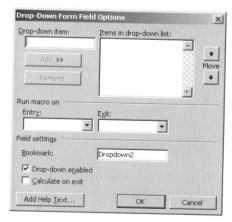

Figure 4-16. *The Drop-Down Form Field Options dialog box*

To remove an item from the drop-down list, highlight it in the box labeled Items in drop-down list. Then click the Remove button. You can reorder items in the drop-down list by highlighting them in the box labeled Items in drop-down list. Then click the arrows labeled Move to move the item up or down in the list.

Once you have made your choices, click OK. On text form fields, you have a number of options. Double-click the text form field to open its properties box, as shown in Figure 4-17.

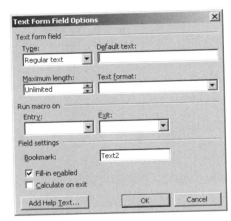

Figure 4-17. *The Text Form Field Options dialog box*

Under Type, you can specify a format, such as a date for the type of text that can be entered in the field. You can also use the Default text box to specify a default entry for the box. Furthermore, you can specify a maximum length for the entry and a format for the text. The format can be used to capitalize the first letter of words or to capitalize the entire entry. Once you have set your options, click OK.

With check boxes, you can change the size of the box in comparison with the size of the surrounding text. Double-click the check box so the Check Box Form Field Options dialog box appears, as shown in Figure 4-18.

You can size the box automatically or specify the size of the box in points.

Furthermore, you can change the default value for the box—checked or unchecked. Finally, click OK. A series of check boxes is not mutually exclusive; users can check as many as are appropriate.

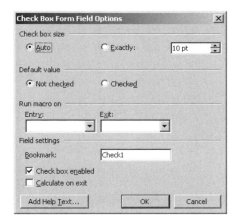

Figure 4-18. *The Check Box Form Field Options dialog box*

Providing Help to Readers

If you anticipate that readers will need help answering questions on the form, you can add help text. Bring up the properties for the form field by clicking the Form Field Options button on the Forms toolbar. Click the Add Help Text button. The Form Field Help Text dialog box, shown in Figure 4-19, will open.

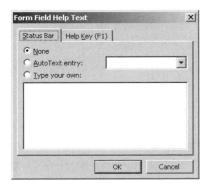

Figure 4-19. *The Form Field Help Text dialog box*

Select either the Status Bar tab or the Help Key (F1) tab. Select Type your own, enter the help text in the box below, then click OK. Status bar help text appears in the status bar when a user clicks a form field. To access other help text, the user must press the F1 key.

Additional Form Options

The property boxes for forms also give you the option of specifying macros to run when a selection is made. This can be used to expand the form, for example, or to make other selections on the form. But for this option to work, you must first create a macro and attach it to the form document. Then you can select the macro in the form field options dialog box. It can be activated when a user accesses or exits a form field. Use the Entry and Exit drop-down boxes in the form field options dialog box to select your macro.

You can also add ActiveX controls to a form for greater control. To access the Control Toolbox, shown in Figure 4-20, right-click in the toolbar area and select Control Toolbox.

Figure 4-20. *The Control Toolbox*

You will find a number of options such as radio and toggle buttons, list buttons, and scroll bars. While many of these can be handy for advanced forms, they require a knowledge of Visual Basic for Applications in order to function correctly.

Protecting and Distributing Your Form

As with printed forms, you should lock your form once you have completed creating it. This will prevent changes to the layout, while users can still complete fields.

If the form is to be distributed electronically, don't forget to save it as a template first. Then each user can open a document and complete the form without saving their changes with the original document.

When one is filling out a form, it is possible to reset all form fields to their default. Simply click the Reset Form Fields button on the Forms toolbar.

■ ■ ■

CHAPTER 5

Creating Legal Documents

The formatting for legal filings may vary depending on the type of filing, but most will use similar elements. You can alter the formatting to suit your unique needs.

A sample legal document is available with the downloads for this book at the Apress web site (http://www.apress.com).

Specifying Page Setup

Before you enter the body text, you should specify the page setup for the entire document. You may later need to alter the page setup in specific parts of your legal filing. Or you may already know that the page setup will differ in certain areas. This is okay. For now, you are setting the predominant page layout for your document.

Access the Page Setup dialog box by clicking File ➤ Page Setup. Click the Margins tab to open the settings for the margins, as shown in Figure 5-1.

The default settings for the Normal.dot template are 1 inch at the top and bottom of the page and 1.25 inches at either side of the page, which is appropriate for most legal documents. However, you can enter new margin sizes if you wish.

Next, click the Paper tab in the Page Setup dialog box (see Figure 5-2). In the Paper size section, use the drop-down box to specify the paper size.

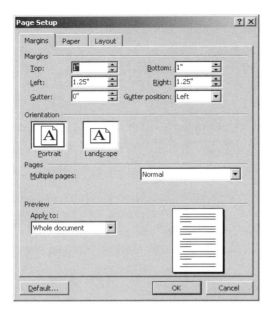

Figure 5-1. *The Margins tab of the Page Setup dialog box*

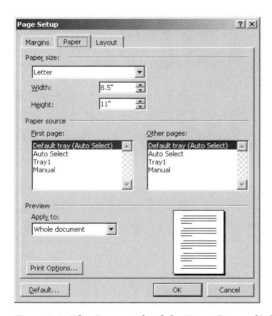

Figure 5-2. *The Paper tab of the Page Setup dialog box*

Use the boxes in the Paper source section to specify the printer's paper tray(s) for the first page of the legal filing and for the subsequent pages. In the Preview section, opt to apply the changes to the whole document.

Click the Print Options button to review the settings, as you see in Figure 5-3. Deselect Draft output if it has been selected. You should select Drawing objects.

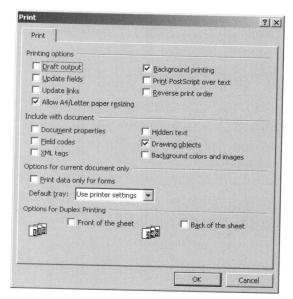

Figure 5-3. *Print options*

Once you have made your selections, click OK.

Entering the Body Text

With legal filings, you need to begin by entering information on the court, the court case, and the parties involved.

First, enter the court information. Then highlight it and click the Bold button on the Formatting toolbar. You will also want to align the information horizontally by clicking the Center button on the Formatting toolbar.

Next, you will need to enter the case number. Highlight the number and then click the Right button on the Formatting toolbar to right align it.

■Tip If you don't see the alignment buttons on the Formatting toolbar, you can display them by clicking the arrow on the right side of the toolbar. Then on the pop-up menu, select Add or Remove Buttons ➤ Formatting, and select the alignment buttons you want.

When you enter information on the parties involved, you may need to have it appear in two columns. There are two ways to do this. First, you can use Word's columns feature.

Using Word's Columns Feature

The easiest way to apply columns to a portion of your document is to use the Columns button on the Standard toolbar. Select a portion of your document and click the button. A drop-down menu allows you to divide the section into a maximum of four columns, as you see in Figure 5-4 (note, however, that if you hold the left mouse button and drag to the right, you are given the option of adding six columns). Highlight two columns to create the two columns in your document.

Figure 5-4. *Inserting columns using the Columns toolbar button*

This doesn't give you many choices. For more advanced options, click Format ➤ Columns. The Columns dialog box opens, as shown in Figure 5-5.

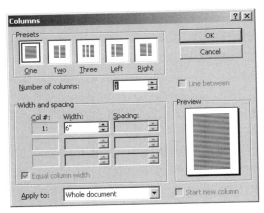

Figure 5-5. *The Columns dialog box*

By default, Word makes each column identical in width. But you can set the width for each column independently. Deselect Equal column width. Then use the controls to specify width, in inches, for each column. The Spacing boxes let you set the distance between the columns.

At the bottom of the first column, insert a column break by clicking Insert ➤ Break to bring up the Break dialog box shown in Figure 5-6. Select Column break and then click OK.

Figure 5-6. *The Break dialog box*

At the bottom of the second column, insert a section break by clicking Insert ➤ Break. Select Continuous and then click OK. Text following the break will remain on the same page. You can work on the rest of the document.

Formatting Columns Using Indents

For legal filings, Word's columns feature can be cumbersome. You can opt to use tabs to create the columns instead.

On the first line, enter the information you would like to appear in the first column. Then set a tab stop by clicking the Ruler. This will be the location where the second column begins. A small black *L* will appear on the Ruler, indicating the tab stop, as shown in Figure 5-7.

Figure 5-7. *Word's Ruler showing a tab stop*

If you need, you can move a tab stop by clicking it and sliding it on the Ruler. To remove a tab stop, click it and drag it off the Ruler.

Tip If you can't see the Ruler, click View ➤ Ruler. The Ruler will appear at the top of the Word window, below the toolbars.

To enter information in the second column, simply press the Tab key once. The cursor will move to the second column, and you can enter text.

Note Tab stops will persist from line to line unless you change them. So I recommend removing or changing the tab stops after you enter the information on the parties involved in the legal case. Otherwise, you may run into problems in later portions of the document.

Setting Line Spacing

For the body of the legal filing, you will likely want the line spacing set to double spacing. This will make the document easier to read.

To set line spacing, right-click where you would like the double line spacing to begin. On the pop-up menu, select Paragraph. Open the Indents and Spacing tab, as shown in Figure 5-8. In the drop-down box labeled Line spacing, select Double. Click OK.

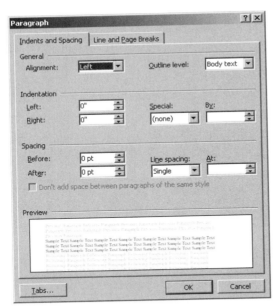

Figure 5-8. *The Indents and Spacing tab of the Paragraph dialog box*

Note Formatting you apply at the paragraph level will continue from paragraph to paragraph—that is, unless you change the paragraph formatting.

Line Numbering

Line numbering will help you refer to specific portions of the document. Word will number each line of text in the left margin of the document. You have a great deal of flexibility when working with line numbering. But your needs will probably be fairly simple in comparison to your options.

To activate line numbering, click File ➤ Page Setup. Open the Layout tab and click Line Numbers to bring up the Line Numbers dialog box, as shown in Figure 5-9. Select Add line numbering. Click OK twice to close the dialog boxes and apply the line numbering.

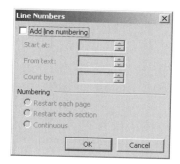

Figure 5-9. *The Line Numbers dialog box*

Figure 5-10 shows how line numbers might look in a legal document.

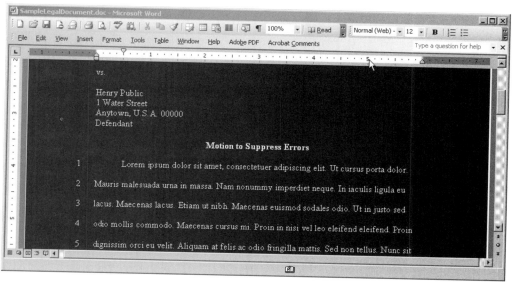

Figure 5-10. *Line numbering in a legal document*

■**Note** Line numbers will appear only in Print Layout view. If you can't see line numbers, switch to Print Layout view by clicking View ➤ Print Layout. Or, you can use the View buttons in the lower left of the Word window.

Since line numbering is applied at the page level, it can be tricky to work with the line numbers. If you followed the preceding steps, you will notice that the parties' information also contains line numbers. You will want to change this.

The process can be a bit tedious, but you can solve the problem. First, insert a section break before the body of the document by clicking Insert ➤ Break. Select Continuous and click OK.

Next, follow the preceding directions for adding line numbering. In the Line Numbers dialog box, select Restart each section. Now, you will notice that the numbering begins at 1 where you created the section break. However, the numbering remains next to the information on the parties.

To remove the line numbers, highlight the lines. Right-click and select Paragraph. Open the Line and Page Breaks tab, as shown in Figure 5-11. Select Suppress line numbers and click OK.

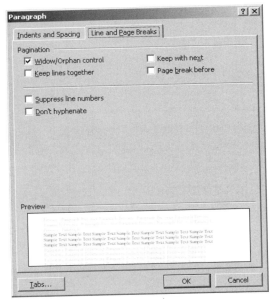

Figure 5-11. *The Line and Page Breaks tab of the Paragraph dialog box*

You will probably want to suppress line numbers in other portions of your document as well. Simply follow the same steps.

Inserting Block Quotes

It is likely you will need to include quotes in your filing. And chances are you would want them to appear in block format.

It is more efficient to enter the quotes with the rest of your document and then format them later. That way, you maintain consistent formatting throughout the document without having to make changes to the paragraph formatting several times.

With block quotes, you need to indent both the left and right margins of the text. Additionally, you should change the line spacing back to single spacing.

First, highlight the quote. Then use the Indent sliders on the Ruler to change the margins. Simply click the square below the pointers on the left side of the Ruler and slide it to the desired position, as shown in Figure 5-12. Half an inch from the current indent is good, although you may wish to increase or decrease the amount of space.

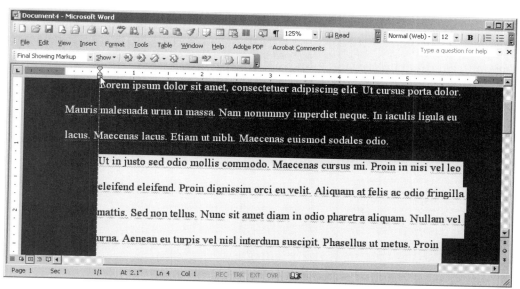

Figure 5-12. *Using the Indent sliders on Word's Ruler*

To increase the right indent, click the pointer on the right side of the Ruler and slide it to the desired position.

Next, change the line spacing by right-clicking the highlighted block of text. Select Paragraph and open the Indents and Spacing tab. Under Line spacing, select Single and click OK.

Note You can also use the Paragraph formatting dialog box to set the right and left indents. However, the sliders on the Ruler are often easier, as a dashed line appears, showing you the position of the indent. You can instantly judge how your document will look without having to guess.

Creating Bulleted or Numbered Lists

There is a good chance that you will want to use bulleted or numbered lists in your document. These types of lists are notoriously difficult to work with in Word, although over the years Word has significantly improved the way it handles lists.

Word generally tries to create a list if you begin a paragraph with a number or a symbol. When you end the paragraph by pressing Return or Enter, it will AutoFormat the paragraph using a list style.

This AutoFormatting is frustrating for many users, particularly if a list is not desirable. And, if you have multiple paragraphs within a list item, it can be difficult to have Word format the list correctly.

I generally recommend that people disable lists in Word's AutoFormat section. This will alleviate much of the frustration. To do this, click Tools ➤ AutoCorrect Options. On the AutoFormat As You Type tab, shown in Figure 5-13, deselect Automatic bulleted lists and Automatic numbered lists.

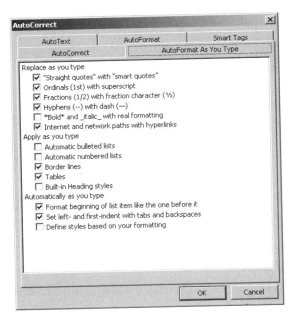

Figure 5-13. *The AutoFormat As You Type tab*

On the AutoFormat tab, shown in Figure 5-14, deselect Automatic bulleted lists and List styles. Click OK.

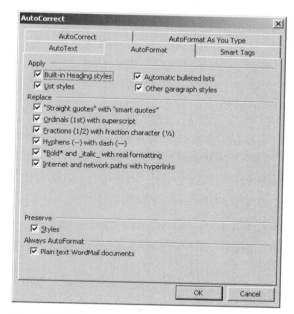

Figure 5-14. *The AutoFormat tab*

Now you can create the lists as you would like by inserting numbers or symbols for list items. Then you can adjust the indents as you please. For some, creating lists manually is preferable to messing around with Word's lists feature. However, keep in mind that lists won't automatically update when individual list items are moved or deleted.

But, for short lists, it is much easier to let Word create the list for you. To begin a list, simply click either the Bullets or Numbering button on the Formatting toolbar.

When you create a list using the toolbar buttons, it is best to allow Word to format the list automatically. Then if you want to make changes to the format, you can do so in one fell swoop when the list is complete.

To change the format of a bulleted list, double-click one of the bullet points. The Bullets and Numbering dialog box opens to the Bulleted tab, as shown in Figure 5-15. There are a number of predefined list formats from which you can choose. Simply highlight one of the styles and click OK.

Or, you can customize a list style by clicking the Customize button. In the Customize Bulleted List dialog box, you have a number of options, as you see in Figure 5-16. You can select from one of the existing bullet characters by selecting it. Or you can select a different symbol by clicking the Character button. The Font button allows you to change a bullet symbol's font.

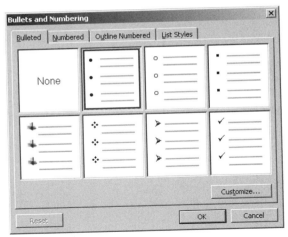

Figure 5-15. *The Bulleted tab of the Bullets and Numbering dialog box*

Figure 5-16. *The Customize Bulleted List dialog box*

In the Bullet position section, use the control box to select the indentation for the character. The Text position section changes the position of the text relative to the left margin. Tab space after sets the position of the first line of text. Indent at changes the position of all subsequent lines.

Once you have made your changes, click OK on each of the open dialog boxes.

To change the formatting of a numbered list, double-click one of the numbers. The Bullets and Numbering dialog box will open to the Numbered tab, as shown in Figure 5-17.

Again, Word gives you the option of selecting from a predefined format. Select one and click OK to apply it. Or, you can click Customize to make changes.

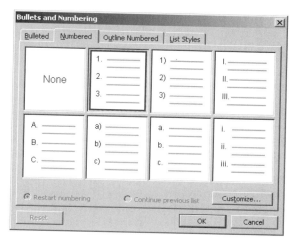

Figure 5-17. *The Numbered tab of the Bullets and Numbering dialog box*

In the Number format box of the Customize Numbered List dialog box, shown in Figure 5-18, you can enter a number and a character, if you want a special format. The Font button provides a way for you to change the font format for the list numbers. You can use the Number style box and the Start at box to apply a specific style of numbering and to change the number at which the list will start.

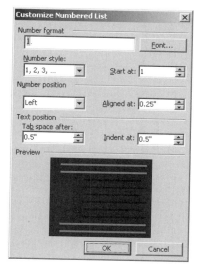

Figure 5-18. *The Customize Numbered List dialog box*

Tip If you are continuing a previous list, don't use the Start at option to change the list. If you delete an earlier list item, the current list won't automatically update. Rather, use the Continue previous list option in the Bullets and Numbering dialog box.

In the Number position section, use the control box to select the indentation for the number. The Text position section changes the position of the text relative to the left margin. Tab space after sets the position of the first line of text. Indent at changes the position of all subsequent lines.

Once you have made your changes, click OK in each of the open dialog boxes.

If you want to remove a bullet point or number from a paragraph, simply position the cursor before the first character in the paragraph text, then press the Backspace key. The bullet or number will be removed; the rest of the list updates automatically.

At the end of a list, press Enter or Return twice to turn off bullets and numbering and to return to a normal paragraph style.

■ ■ ■

CHAPTER 6

Creating Data Sheets

Data sheets often require intricate formatting. In addition to text, you will want to include bulleted lists enumerating product features and diagrams of specific components. Fortunately, Word has features that will simplify the process of creating your data sheet.

You can see a sample data sheet with the downloads for this book at the Apress web site (http://www.apress.com).

Specifying Page Setup

Before you enter any text or diagrams, specify the page setup for the entire document. You may decide later to alter the page setup in specific parts of your data sheet. Or, you may already know that the page setup will differ in certain areas. This is okay. For now, you are setting the predominant page layout for your document.

Access the Page Setup dialog box by clicking File ➤ Page Setup. Click the Margins tab to open the settings for the margins, as shown in Figure 6-1.

The default settings for the Normal.dot template are 1 inch at the top and bottom of the page and 1.25 inches at either side of the page. You can enter new margin sizes if you wish.

Next, click the Paper tab in the Page setup dialog box (see Figure 6-2). In the Paper size section, use the drop-down box to specify the paper size.

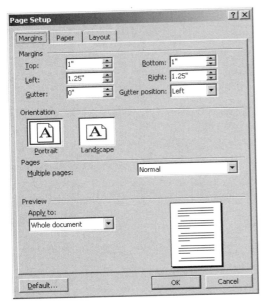

Figure 6-1. *The Margins tab of the Page Setup dialog box*

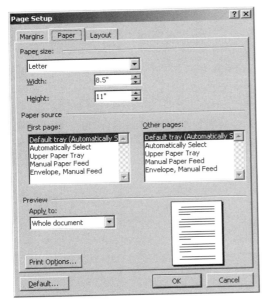

Figure 6-2. *The Paper tab of the Page Setup dialog box*

Use the boxes in the Paper source section to specify the printer's paper tray(s) for the first page of the data sheet and for the subsequent pages. In the Preview section, opt to apply the changes to the whole document.

Click the Print Options button to review the settings, as shown in Figure 6-3. Deselect Draft output if it has been selected. You should select Drawing objects.

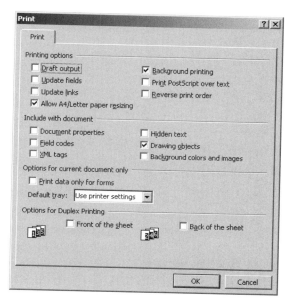

Figure 6-3. *The Print dialog box*

Once you have made your selections, click OK.

On the Layout tab, shown in Figure 6-4, check the document's vertical alignment. Select the alignment in the drop-down box. Opt to apply the changes to the whole document or from that point forward, then click OK.

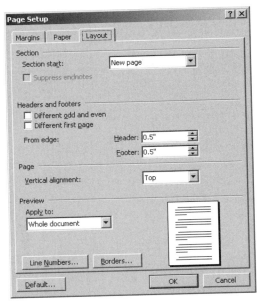

Figure 6-4. *The Layout tab of the Page Setup dialog box*

Inserting Columns in Your Data Sheet

Columns can help you arrange product features neatly. Combined with bulleted lists, they will lend a refined look to your document. However, columns can be tricky if you don't use them correctly. But when you understand a few key points, they're relatively simple.

The easiest way to apply columns to a portion of your document is to use the Columns button on the Standard toolbar. Select a portion of your document and click the button. A drop-down menu gives you the option of dividing the section into four columns, as you see in Figure 6-5. However, if you hold the left mouse button and drag to the right, you are given the option of adding six columns. Simply highlight the number of columns you want to apply.

Figure 6-5. *Creating columns using the Columns toolbar button*

This doesn't give you many choices. For more advanced options, click Format ➤ Columns.

You can select from the Presets column designs shown in Figure 6-6. Or, you can specify the number of columns you want by using the Number of columns box. Word supports up to 12 columns.

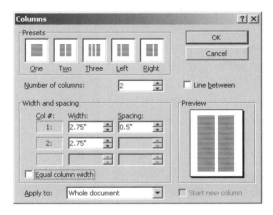

Figure 6-6. *The Columns dialog box*

By default, Word makes each column identical in width. But you can set the width for each column independently. Deselect Equal column width. Then use the controls to specify width, in inches, for each column. The Spacing boxes let you set the distance between the columns.

If you would like a line between each column, select Line between. Use the Preview section to see how your columns will look.

■**Tip** For greater control over the appearance of columns, you can insert column breaks. This will push all text after the break into the next column, so you won't need to enter returns to move text. To insert a column break, click Insert ➤ Break. Select Column break and click OK.

Finally, choose Selected text in the Apply to drop-down box. Or, you can select Whole document to apply it to the entire document. If text isn't selected, your choices are This point forward or Whole document. Click OK.

■**Caution** Columns can become problematic in some situations. That's because Word must create a new section when you change the number of columns in your document. So keep this in mind if you're working with other elements that change from section to section.

Creating Bulleted Lists

There is a good chance that you will want to use bulleted lists in your data sheet. Although they are a handy way to list product features and specifications, these types of lists are notoriously difficult to work with in Word. However, recently Word has significantly improved the way it handles lists.

Word generally tries to create a list if you begin a paragraph with a number or a symbol. When you end the paragraph by pressing Return or Enter, it will AutoFormat the paragraph in a list style.

This AutoFormatting is frustrating for many users, particularly if a list is not desirable. And, if you have multiple paragraphs within a list item, it can be difficult to have Word format the list correctly.

I generally recommend that people disable lists in Word's AutoFormat section, which will alleviate much of the frustration. To do this, click Tools ➤ AutoCorrect Options. On the AutoFormat As You Type tab, shown in Figure 6-7, deselect Automatic bulleted lists and Automatic numbered lists.

Figure 6-7. *The AutoFormat As You Type tab of the AutoCorrect dialog box*

On the AutoFormat tab, shown in Figure 6-8, deselect Automatic bulleted lists and List styles. Click OK.

Figure 6-8. *The AutoFormat tab of the AutoCorrect dialog box*

Now you can create the lists as you would like by inserting symbols for list items. Then you can adjust the indents as you would like. For some, creating lists manually is preferable to messing around with Word's lists feature. However, keep in mind that such lists won't automatically update when individual list items are moved or deleted.

But, for short lists, it is much easier to let Word create the list for you. To begin a list, simply click the Bullets button on the Formatting toolbar.

When you create a list using the toolbar buttons, it is best to allow Word to format the list automatically. Then if you want to make changes to the format, you can do so in one fell swoop when the list is complete.

To change the format of a bulleted list, double-click one of the bullet points. The Bullets and Numbering dialog box opens (see Figure 6-9). There are a number of predefined list formats from which you can choose. Simply highlight one of the styles and click OK.

Or, you can customize a list style by clicking the Customize button. In the Customize Bulleted List dialog box, shown in Figure 6-10, you have a number of options. You can choose from one of the existing bullet characters by selecting it, or you can choose a different symbol by clicking the Character button. The Font button allows you to change the bullet symbol's font.

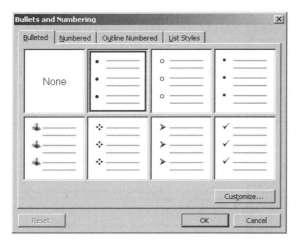

Figure 6-9. *The Bullets and Numbering dialog box*

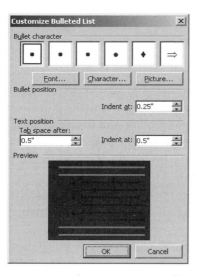

Figure 6-10. *The Customize Bulleted List dialog box*

In the Bullet position section, use the control box to select the indentation for the character. The Text position section changes the position of the text relative to the left margin. Tab space after sets the position of the first line of text. Indent at changes the position of all subsequent lines.

Once you have made your changes, click OK in each of the open dialog boxes.

If you want to remove a bullet point or number from a paragraph, simply position the cursor before the first character in the paragraph text, then press the Backspace key. The bullet will be removed; the rest of the list updates automatically.

At the end of a list, press Enter or Return twice to turn off bullets and to return to a normal paragraph style.

Inserting Pictures

Images are an important part of data sheets. You can insert diagrams and other images into a Word document in a few simple steps. And Word provides you with a number of options for formatting them perfectly.

■Note The steps for inserting images are the same no matter where in your document you are placing them. For example, with data sheets you may want to insert a company logo in the document header. Also, you can insert pictures in a table, if you want to align the images neatly.

To insert an image, click Insert ➤ Picture ➤ From File. Navigate through the Insert Picture dialog box, shown in Figure 6-11, to find the correct image. As you can see in the Files of type box, Word accepts a wide variety of image types.

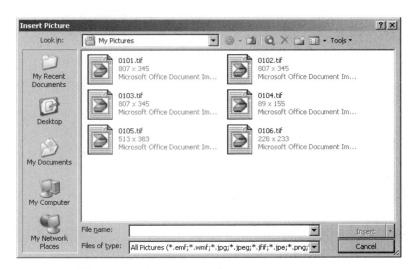

Figure 6-11. *The Insert Picture dialog box*

When you find your image, select it and click Insert. The image will appear at the current cursor position.

It is also possible to insert a picture by copying it from a different program, such as a photo editing program. Then select the place in your document where you want to insert the image and use the Ctrl+V shortcut key to paste the picture into the document.

When you click an image in Word, the Picture toolbar appears (see Figure 6-12). It provides a number of options for editing your picture, such as adjusting brightness, contrast, and color. You can also crop images or rotate them.

Figure 6-12. *The Picture toolbar*

■**Caution** Word provides you with a number of options for editing pictures you insert in your document. I strongly advise that you avoid editing your images in Word. Rather, use a program that is designed specifically for editing images and edit the images before inserting them in the document.

To crop a picture, click the Crop button. A black bar appears on each side of the picture, plus on each corner. Click and drag the bars to move the edge of the picture. When you've made your adjustments, click outside of the picture.

The Text Wrapping button helps you position the picture in relation to the text. Click the button and select an option from the drop-down menu, as shown in Figure 6-13.

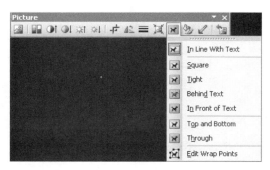

Figure 6-13. *Text wrapping options*

To align your picture in relation to the document margins, select it and then click one of the alignment buttons on the Formatting toolbar.

You can resize the picture by clicking and dragging the black boxes on the edges or in the corners of the picture.

For more advanced formatting options, right-click your picture and select Format Picture to open the Format Picture dialog box.

The Size tab, shown in Figure 6-14, lets you manually set the size of your picture. You can also scale your picture by percentage. To keep the picture proportions, select Lock aspect ratio.

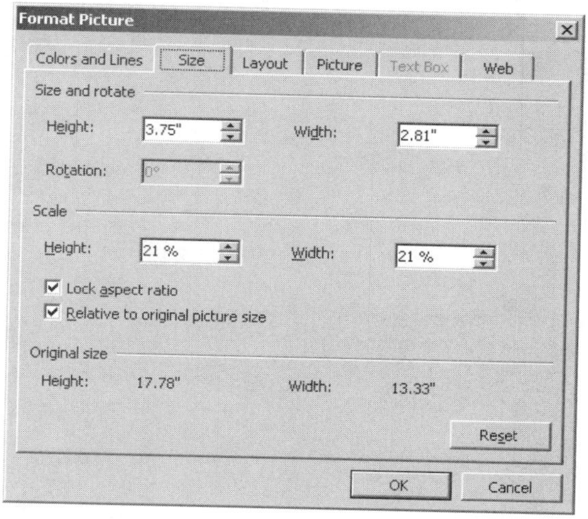

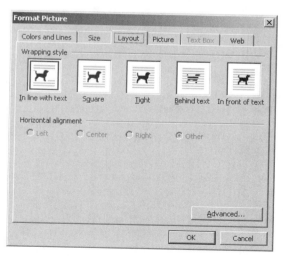

Figure 6-14. *The Size tab of the Format Picture dialog box*

On the Layout tab, shown in Figure 6-15, you can specify text wrapping and horizontal alignment.

Figure 6-15. *The Layout tab of the Format Picture dialog box*

The Advanced button opens the Advanced Layout dialog box. On the Text Wrapping tab, shown in Figure 6-16, you can specify the distance between the picture and text. You can also specify text wrapping for specific sides of the picture.

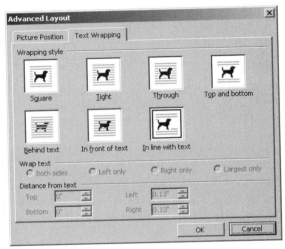

Figure 6-16. *The Text Wrapping tab of the Advanced Layout dialog box*

On the Picture Position tab, select both vertical and horizontal alignment options. You can also set the alignment in relation to specific elements of the document (see Figure 6-17). Once you've made your changes, click OK to return to the Format Picture dialog box.

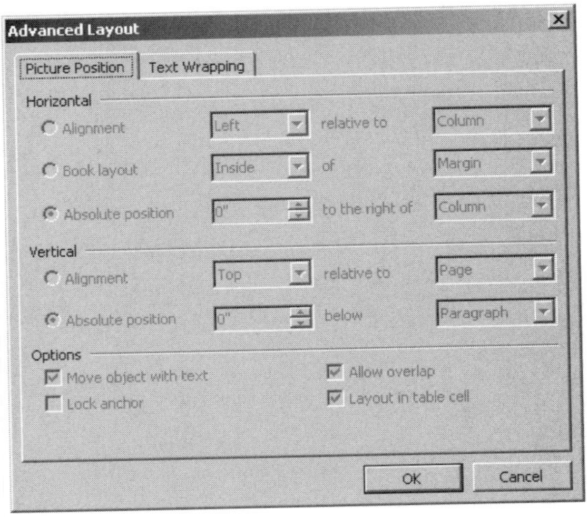

Figure 6-17. *The Picture Position tab of the Advanced Layout dialog box*

On the Picture tab, shown in Figure 6-18, you can specify picture cropping in inches. You can also make changes to the image brightness and contrast.

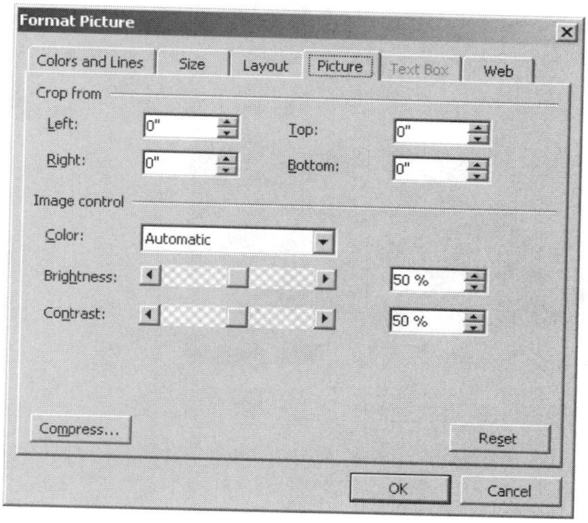

Figure 6-18. *The Picture tab of the Format Picture dialog box*

Inserting a Table

You may not find it necessary to insert a table in your data sheet. However, you might find tables are a handy way to organize diagrams. They can also be used to list technical specifications.

The easiest way for you to create a table in Word is to use the Insert Table button on the Standard toolbar.

Position the cursor where you would like the table placed. Then click the Insert Table button. Use the drop-down grid, shown in Figure 6-19, to select the number of rows and columns for the table. When you release the mouse, Word inserts the table at the appropriate location in your document.

Figure 6-19. *Using the Insert Table button to create a table*

You will notice that tables you create with this method span the entire width of the document, no matter how many columns they contain (see Figure 6-20).

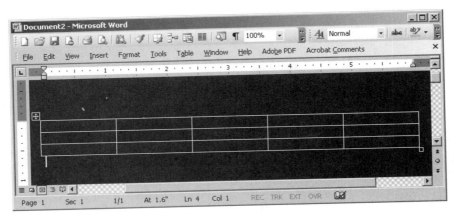

Figure 6-20. *A table created with the Insert Table button*

For more control over your columns, use the Insert Table dialog box, which allows you to specify a number of different formatting options for your table.

To access the Insert Table dialog box, place the cursor where you would like to position the table. Then click Table ➤ Insert ➤ Table. In the Insert Table dialog box, shown in Figure 6-21, specify the number of columns and rows you would like the table to contain. You can also set options for the column width. By default, Word automatically sets the width of the columns. However, you can use the Fixed column width box to specify the width of the columns in inches. Or, you can have Word AutoFit the table to the window or table contents.

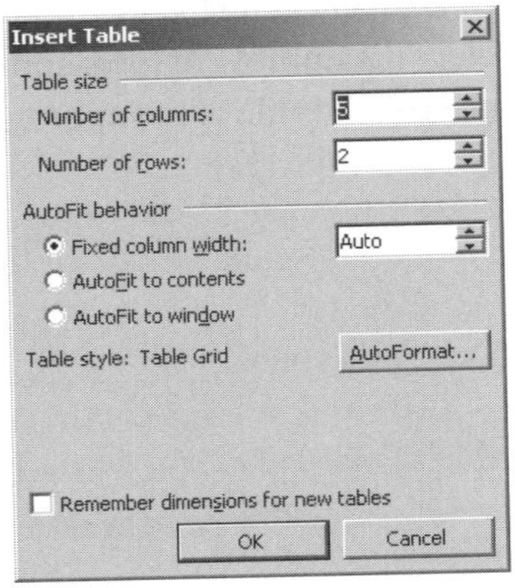

Figure 6-21. *The Insert Table dialog box*

You will notice the AutoFormat button on the Insert Table dialog box. This opens a dialog box that allows you to specify predetermined formats to the table. In the Table AutoFormat dialog box, shown in Figure 6-22, you first select a table style. Word displays the table formatting in the Preview box. At the bottom of the dialog box, you can use the selections to add or remove formatting from specific rows and columns. When you're done, click OK. Then click OK in the Insert Table dialog box.

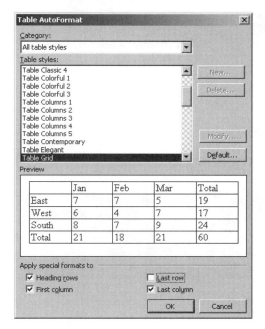

Figure 6-22. *The Table AutoFormat dialog box*

To enter data in the table, simply click in a cell and begin typing. Or, follow the steps for inserting diagrams.

If you decide you want to add more rows or columns to your table, you can do so quite easily. To add a row, click to the left of the row below which you would like to add a new row. Once the row is selected, the Insert Table button on the Standard toolbar changes to the Insert Rows button, as you can see in Figure 6-23.

To add a column, click the border above the column beside which you would like to insert an additional column. The Insert Table button on the Standard toolbar changes to the Insert Columns button. Word inserts the column to the left of the selected column, as Figure 6-24 demonstrates.

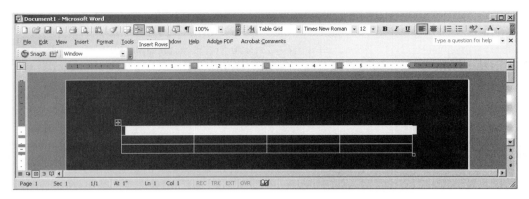

Figure 6-23. *Adding a row to a table*

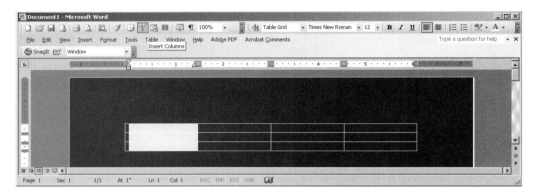

Figure 6-24. *Adding a column to a table*

■**Tip** For more flexibility in choosing where to insert rows and columns, use the Insert submenu on the Table menu instead of the toolbar buttons.

To remove rows or columns, select the row or column you would like to delete. Then click Table ➤ Delete and select what to delete.

Modifying a Table's Layout

After you've created your table, you can make changes to the layout if you need. You can resize the columns and rows by clicking and dragging the borders. Also, you can merge or split cells as you would in Excel.

To merge cells, select the rows or columns you would like to combine. Then on the Table menu, click Merge Cells, as shown in Figure 6-25.

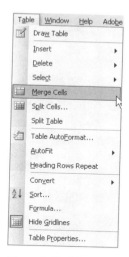

Figure 6-25. *Merging table cells*

To split cells, select the row or column you would like to divide, and click Table ➤ Split Cells. In the Split Cells dialog box, shown in Figure 6-26, specify the number of rows or columns you would like to create. After you've specified the options, click OK.

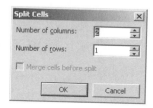

Figure 6-26. *The Split Cells dialog box*

Formatting Tables

If you didn't specify an AutoFormat when you created your table, or if you want to change the format you applied, you can still format your table.

To apply formatting to the character in your table, select the text and use the buttons on the Formatting toolbar to change character attributes.

If you want to change text alignment or table alignment, or apply borders and shading, you'll need to use the Table Properties dialog box, shown in Figure 6-27. You can access this by selecting a portion of your table, right-clicking, and selecting Table Properties.

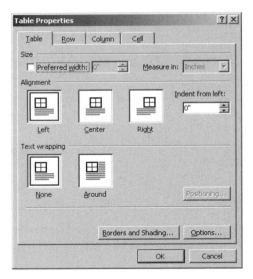

Figure 6-27. *The Table Properties dialog box*

To change text alignment, open the Cell tab, shown in Figure 6-28, and specify text alignment properties. You can choose top, center, or bottom. If you want to change text wrapping within cells, click the Options button. Specify whether you want text to wrap to the next line or to fit on one line. Click OK.

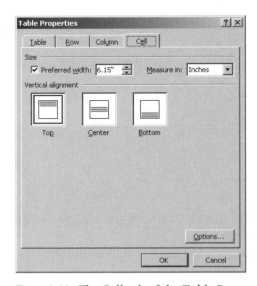

Figure 6-28. *The Cell tab of the Table Properties dialog box*

To change the table alignment, open the Table tab in the Table Properties dialog box, as shown in Figure 6-29. Select how you want Word to align the table on the page. For more control, you can specify a left indentation for the table.

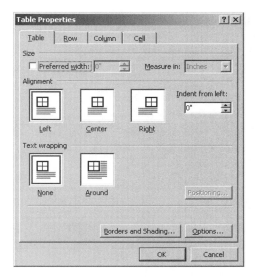

Figure 6-29. *The Table tab of the Table Properties dialog box*

You also have the option of wrapping document text around the table. For business plans, you should turn text wrapping off.

You can specify margins for text within the cell and padding between the cells. This allows you to space your data nicely across the page. To access these controls, click the Options button to bring up the Table Options dialog box, as shown in Figure 6-30.

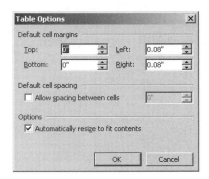

Figure 6-30. *Options for specifying cell margins and padding*

If you want to add borders or shading to cells, click the Borders and Shading button in the Table Properties dialog box.

On the Borders tab, shown in Figure 6-31, select the border style, color, and width. There are border presets that will apply the border style you choose to specific areas of the table. Or, you can click in the diagram on the right to specify where you want the borders to appear.

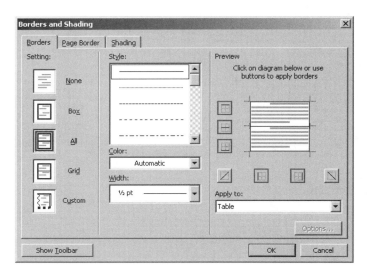

Figure 6-31. *Adding borders to a table*

To specify shading, open the Shading tab, as shown in Figure 6-32. Select the color you would like to apply from the color chart. For more options, click More Colors. In the Patterns section, you can select a shading pattern. Finally, click OK.

To change a table that you've AutoFormatted, click in the table. Click Table ➤ Table AutoFormat. In the Table AutoFormat dialog box, click Modify. In the Modify Style dialog box, shown in Figure 6-33, enter a new name for the table style. Then use the controls to change the table formats. When you're done, click OK. Then close the Table AutoFormat dialog box.

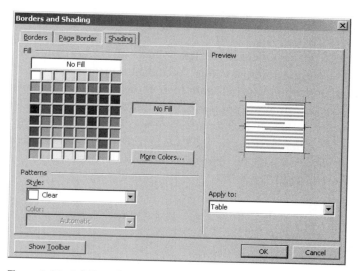

Figure 6-32. *Adding shading to table cells*

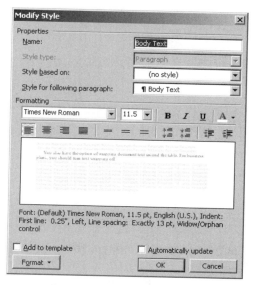

Figure 6-33. *The Modify Style dialog box*

Working with Headers and Footers

You should add a header and footer to your data sheet. The header can contain information, such as a product name and company information. You can also insert logos or drawing objects in the header. In the footer, you will want to include information such as a page number, document version information, and a creation date.

To insert headers and footers, click View ➤ Header and Footer. Click the Page Setup button on the Header and Footer toolbar to bring up the Page Setup dialog box shown in Figure 6-34. Use the controls to specify the distance from the edge of the paper. In the Preview section, select This point forward. Click OK.

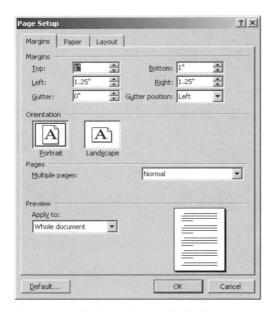

Figure 6-34. *The Page Setup dialog box*

Scroll down and click within the footer box. On the Formatting toolbar, click the right alignment button. Then on the Header and Footer toolbar, click the Insert Page Number button. Click the Format Page Number button. In the Page Number Format box, select the number format.

Scroll down and click within the footer box. On the Formatting toolbar, click the right alignment button. Then on the Header and Footer toolbar, click the Insert Page Number button. Click the Format Page Number button. In the Page Number Format box, select the number format. You should select standard numbering. Under Page numbering, select Start at and use the controls to select the appropriate page number. Click OK.

CHAPTER 7

Creating Organization Charts

Organization charts are a handy way to show the relationship between workers in an organization, departments within a company, or other related material.

You may be tempted to use the drawing tools to make your organization chart, but Word has a built-in tool that will make it for you. This tool offers a high level of customization and is much easier than using drawing tools, which are better suited for flow charts.

A sample organization chart is available with the downloads for this book at the Apress web site (http://www.apress.com).

Inserting an Organization Chart

To create an organization chart, place the cursor where you would like to insert the chart. It can be in a separate document, or you can insert it within another document. On the Insert menu, select Picture ➤ Organization Chart (see Figure 7-1).

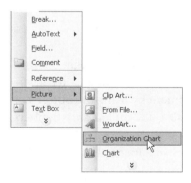

Figure 7-1. *Inserting an organization chart*

As you see in Figure 7-2, Word will insert a basic organization chart with one top-level box and three subordinate levels. Additionally, the Organization Chart toolbar opens.

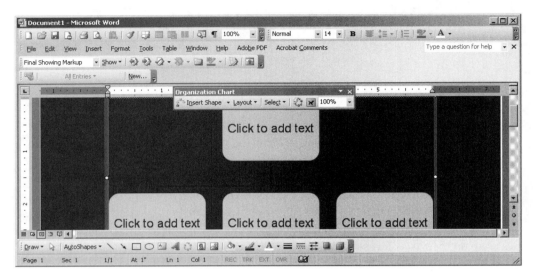

Figure 7-2. *A basic organization chart*

As the figure shows, there are only a few parts to an organization chart: the shapes that hold a person, process, or department; the connector lines that connect the shapes, showing relationships; and the frame that surrounds the chart.

Adding Text to Chart Boxes

You can begin by adding text to the existing boxes. Click within a box and begin typing. The placeholder text that first appears will disappear when you start typing. You can format the text as you would in any other part of your document by using the buttons on the Formatting toolbar. You can change the font color and size, add bullets and numbers, add highlights, and change the alignment within the box.

For more advanced options, right-click in the box and select Paragraph, as shown in Figure 7-3. This will give you more options for the way the text appears within the box. Or, select Font to specify more detailed options for the font itself.

Figure 7-3. *The context menu*

Inserting Pictures

When you're adding text to a box in an organization chart, you can also add images—this can be especially helpful when you are creating charts of a department.

To insert an image, click Insert ➤ Picture ➤ From File. Navigate through the Insert Picture dialog box, shown in Figure 7-4, to find the correct image. Word accepts a wide variety of image types.

Figure 7-4. *The Insert Picture dialog box*

When you find your image, select it and click Insert. The image will appear at the current cursor position.

It is also possible to insert a picture by copying it from a different program, such as a photo editing program. Select the place in your document where you want to insert the image, then use the Ctrl+V shortcut key to paste the picture into the document.

Editing Pictures

When you click an image in Word, the Picture toolbar appears, as shown in Figure 7-5. It provides a number of options for editing your picture, such as adjusting brightness, contrast, and color. You can also crop images or rotate them.

Figure 7-5. *The Picture toolbar*

■**Caution** Word provides you with a number of options for editing pictures you insert in your document. I strongly advise that you avoid editing your images in Word. Rather, you should use a program that is designed specifically for editing images and edit the images before inserting them in the document for two reasons. First, you'll get better images. Second, you won't end up with a bloated file.

To crop a picture, click the Crop button. A black bar appears on each side of the picture, plus on each corner. Click and drag the bars to move the edge of the picture. When you've made your adjustments, click outside of the picture.

The Text Wrapping button helps you position the picture in relation to the text. Click the button and select an option from the drop-down menu, as shown in Figure 7-6.

Figure 7-6. *Text wrapping options*

To align your picture in relation to the document margins, select it and then click one of the alignment buttons on the Formatting toolbar.

You can resize the picture by clicking and dragging the black boxes on the edges and/or in the corners of the picture.

For more advanced formatting options, right-click your picture and select Format Picture to open the Format Picture dialog box.

The Size tab, which you see in Figure 7-7, lets you manually set the size of your picture. You can also scale your picture by percentage. To keep the picture proportions, select Lock aspect ratio.

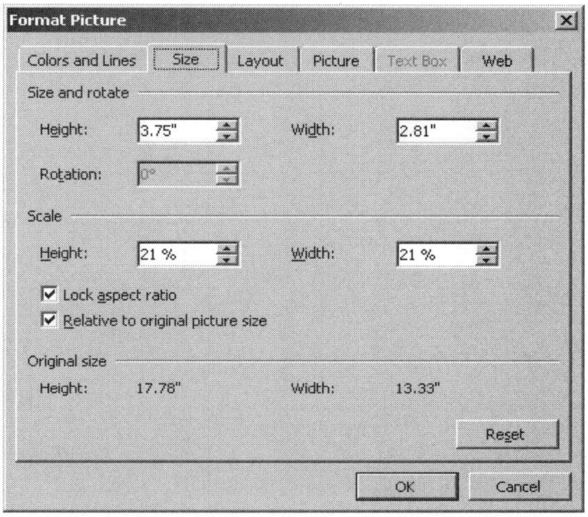

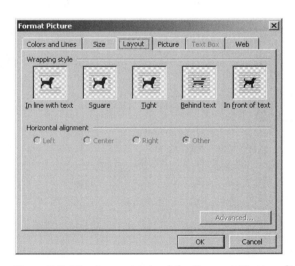

Figure 7-7. *The Size tab of the Format Picture dialog box*

On the Layout tab, shown in Figure 7-8, you can specify text wrapping and horizontal alignment.

Figure 7-8. *The Layout tab of the Format Picture dialog box*

The Advanced button opens the Advanced Layout dialog box. On the Text Wrapping tab, shown in Figure 7-9, you can specify the distance between the picture and text. You can also specify text wrapping for specific sides of the picture.

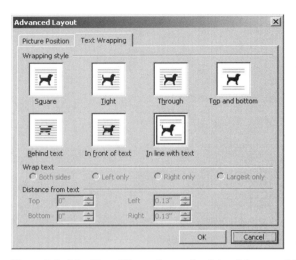

Figure 7-9. *The Text Wrapping tab of the Advanced Layout dialog box*

On the Picture Position tab, shown in Figure 7-10, select both vertical and horizontal alignment options. You can also set the alignment in relation to specific elements of the document. Once you've made your changes, click OK to return to the Format Picture dialog box.

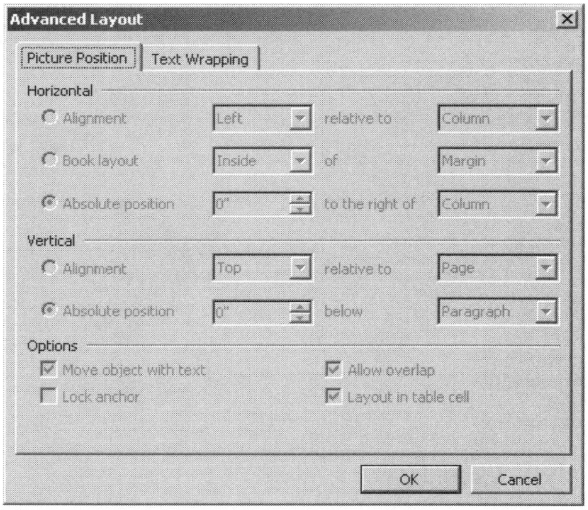

Figure 7-10. *The Picture Position tab of the Advanced Layout dialog box*

On the Picture tab, you can specify picture cropping in inches, as shown in Figure 7-11. You can also make changes to the image brightness and contrast.

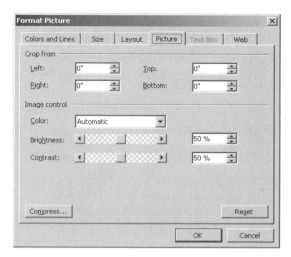

Figure 7-11. *The Picture tab of the Format Picture dialog box*

Formatting Your Organization Chart

You can change attributes of the organization chart by right-clicking the border surrounding the chart. Select Format Organization Chart from the pop-up menu. In the dialog box that appears are several tabs that provide a number of options.

The Colors and Lines tab in the Format Organization Chart dialog box gives you a number of options for formatting the chart (see Figure 7-12). Use the color box to select a background color for the chart area. You can also use the slider or percentage boxes to set the transparency for the background color.

The Line section allows you to specify a color, style, weight, and dash pattern for the chart border. By default, the chart will not have a border line. But it can be helpful to add one, particularly if you are inserting the chart within a document.

The Size tab, shown in Figure 7-13, lets you specify the height and width for the organization chart. Or, you can use the scale tools to adjust the proportions of the organization chart. By default, Lock aspect ratio is selected, but you can deselect it if you do not want to constrain the proportions.

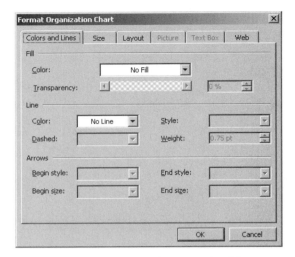

Figure 7-12. *The Colors and Lines tab of the Format Organization Chart dialog box*

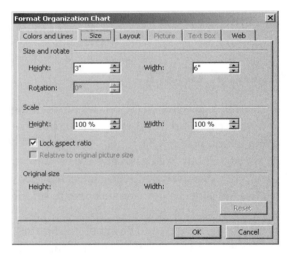

Figure 7-13. *The Size tab of the Format Organization Chart dialog box*

Note You can also use the white dots on the corners and sides of the organization chart to resize the chart.

The Layout tab is useful if you are inserting the chart into a larger document (see Figure 7-14). It specifies how the chart will appear in relation to the text on the rest of the page. Additionally, this tab contains an Advanced button. The options it brings up will give you greater control over how the chart appears in relation to other parts of the document, such as enabling you to specify the amount of space between the chart and text. You can also use the Text Wrapping button on the Organization Chart toolbar to set text wrapping options.

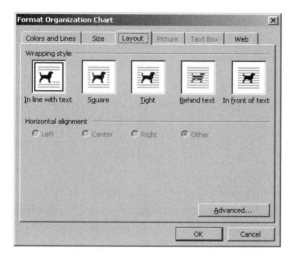

Figure 7-14. *The Layout tab of the Format Organization Chart dialog box*

When you've made your choices, select OK.

Arranging Your Organization Chart

When you're creating your organization chart, it is best to start at the top level and work your way down to the lower levels. While the Insert Shape button allows you to insert more levels, it does not provide a way to insert levels above the top-most level.

To insert a new level, first select the level that will be the reference for the new level or box of the reference chart. Then click the Insert Shape button and on the drop-down list select Subordinate, Coworker, or Assistant, as shown in Figure 7-15. Word will insert the shape at the appropriate position on the chart.

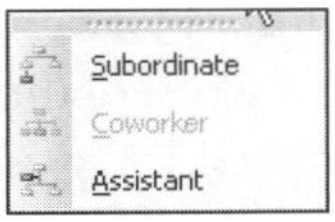

Figure 7-15. *The Insert Shape button's drop-down list*

To change the appearance of the boxes in the chart, use the Layout button to choose a layout for the chart from a list of options for the layout of the chart—the levels can be linear or horizontal. For example, you can have subordinate levels hang to the right or to the left. Or you can have them hang on both sides (see Figure 7-16).

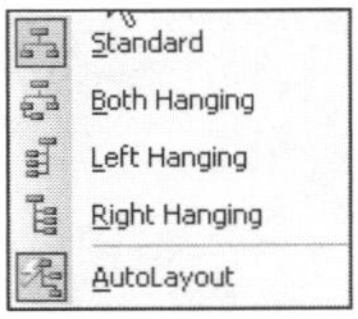

Figure 7-16. *The Layout button's drop-down list*

If you're unsure of the best layout for the table, select the AutoLayout option, as shown in Figure 7-17. It chooses the best layout for the table.

Figure 7-17. *The AutoLayout button*

Finally, you may not like the default style for the organization chart. Fortunately, you are not stuck with Word's default layout. You can use the AutoFormat option to select a different style for the organization chart. Some are contemporary, while others are more traditional. But due to the wide selection, you are sure to find one that suits your needs.

When you click the AutoFormat button, the Organization Chart Style Gallery dialog box opens, giving you many different choices. Click your choice on the left side to view a preview on the right, as shown in Figure 7-18. When you find one you like, click OK. It will change the current chart to match that style.

The Select button on the Organization Chart toolbar will allow you to select different aspects of the chart, such as connecting lines, a level, or a branch (see Figure 7-19). This will allow you to alter the characteristics of the elements or delete them altogether.

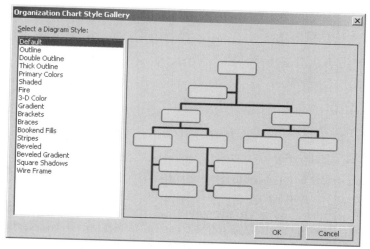

Figure 7-18. *The Organization Chart Style Gallery dialog box*

Figure 7-19. *The Select button's drop-down list*

Rearranging Your Organization Chart

If you want to rearrange the order of boxes within an organization chart, you can move a shape, or even whole sections.

You can click and drag the different boxes within the organization chart. Simply click one and then drag the dotted border surrounding it. Move it to the desired location.

To move entire levels or branches, first select a box at the same level, and use the Select button to select the branch or level. Then drag the entire branch to a new location.

The Text Wrapping button on the toolbar, shown in Figure 7-20, gives you options for wrapping text around the organization chart, but you are better off using the Layout tab from the AutoFormat dialog box for this task.

Figure 7-20. *The Text Wrapping button*

To change the size of a box, click the border so that dots appear at the corners of the box and at the sides, as shown in Figure 7-21.

Figure 7-21. *A selected shape*

If you desire, you can change the colors for the relationship lines and for the individual shapes. Simply right-click the object and select Format AutoShape, as shown in Figure 7-22. Use the Colors and Lines tab to make changes to the colors and borders of the shapes and lines. To apply the same changes to all the boxes or lines, use the Select button to select the relationship lines, branch, or level. Then use the Format AutoShape options to make your changes.

Figure 7-22. *The Format AutoShape context menu option*

For added flexibility, you can add subordinates, coworkers, and assistants by right-clicking a shape and selecting the type you would like to add from the same context menu shown in Figure 7-22. The context menu also gives you the option of changing the layout of a sublevel or deleting a box from the organization chart.

Adding Captions to Your Organization Chart

You may want to add a caption to your organization chart, as it helps you identify the chart when you refer to it in your document.

To insert a caption, select your chart. Click Insert ➤ Reference ➤ Caption. In the Label box, select the type of label. Then specify the position of the label. Enter the caption text in the box labeled Caption, as shown in Figure 7-23. Finally, click OK.

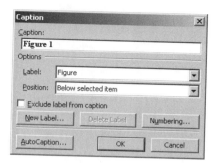

Figure 7-23. *The Caption dialog box*

Word inserts the caption as a field. The numbering updates automatically if you add more captions or rearrange captioned objects.

Once you have created and formatted your organization chart, you can incorporate it into an existing document by copying and pasting. Or, you can add text to the file containing the organization chart.

■ ■ ■

CHAPTER 8

Creating a Grant or Business Proposal

The many different sections and variety of information contained in a business proposal make its formatting an intricate process. But by planning the document before you start creating it, you will simplify the process.

A sample business proposal is available with the downloads for this book at the Apress web site (http://www.apress.com).

Getting Started with Word's Outline View

If your business proposal is lengthy, it's best to start with an outline. This is particularly true if you need to include a table of contents. The outline will allow you to organize the different parts of the document, and you will also see at a glance the sections you are including, so you won't inadvertently omit a portion of the document. The outline levels will help you create a table of contents that updates automatically as the document evolves.

With Word's Outline view, you can create an outline with ease. To switch to Outline view, click the View menu and select Outline. The Outline view differs substantially from other document views. You will also notice that the Outlining toolbar appears below the Standard and Formatting toolbars, as shown in Figure 8-1. It contains a number of options that will help you work with your outline.

Note When you change document views, you may not see certain elements of your document. Also, with the exception of Print Layout view, the document views do not accurately represent how your finished document will appear. Keep this in mind as you work. If you need to gauge how your finished document will look, you can toggle back and forth between document views via the View menu or the view buttons in the lower left of the Word window. The Print Preview button on the Standard toolbar also shows you how your document will look.

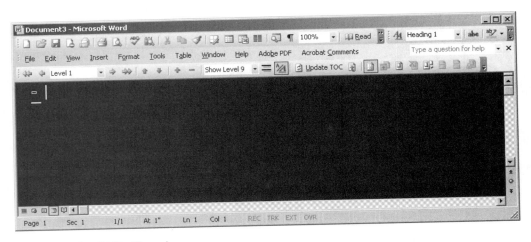

Figure 8-1. *Word's Outline view*

In Outline view, enter each section heading on a new line. You should also enter headings for the subsections. Notice that a small minus sign appears in the left margin of each line.

Once you have entered the section headings and subsection headings, you are ready to assign each heading a level. Think of it as a standard outline, even though you might not use Roman numerals, numbers, and letters.

By default, Word assigns each line to Level 1. You will probably find that most of the sections of your business proposal remain at Level 1. However, some sections will require subsections. So you will need to move some sections to a lower level.

There are several ways to change a heading level. The easiest way to do so is to place the cursor at the beginning of the heading. Then use the Tab key to change the level. Press the Tab key once to lower the heading one level. You will notice that the minus sign in the left margin on the preceding level changes to a plus sign, as illustrated in Figure 8-2.

Should you need to promote a heading up a level, press Shift+Tab to move it.

■**Note** When you switch to Print Layout view, you will notice that Word has automatically applied formatting to your document. This is normal. Word uses the heading styles incorporated in the Normal.dot template, the template upon which all blank documents are based. If you do not want to use the default styles, don't worry. The styles can be altered later when you format the document.

The headings subordinate to the heading you move will not move automatically. If you want the subheadings to maintain the same relative position, use the plus sign in the left margin. Click it to highlight the level and its subordinate levels. When you change the level, the relative position of the other levels also changes (see Figure 8-3).

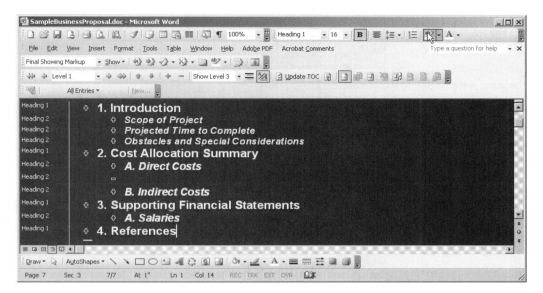

Figure 8-2. *Showing sublevels in Outline view*

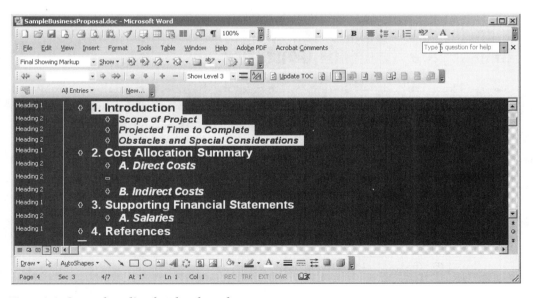

Figure 8-3. *Several outline levels selected*

■**Tip** When working in Outline view, you can expand or collapse a portion of your outline by double-clicking the plus sign in the margin. If you want to collapse your entire outline, use the Outlining toolbar. The Show Level drop-down box allows you to select the levels you would like to view. You can select Levels 1 through 9, as listed in Figure 8-4, or you can opt to show all levels.

Figure 8-4. *The Show Level drop-down box on the Outlining toolbar*

If you need to change the order of one of the headings, click the plus or minus sign in the margin. Then drag it to the correct location. When you move a level, you will also move the sublevels that have been highlighted.

Creating a Table of Contents

Once you have created your outline, you're ready for the table of contents. You may find it counterintuitive to create the table of contents before the rest of the document. When you create a table of contents manually, it makes sense to insert it when the document is finalized. That way, you don't need to worry about updating page numbers.

Word will create a table of contents automatically. By using this feature, you will avoid the problems associated with creating one manually. First, Word uses the headings you entered in Outline view to create the table of contents. You won't need to waste time entering the information a second time.

Word also makes it easy to format the table, providing several predefined options. But, best of all, Word will automatically update the page numbering for you. So, as your document grows in length, the table of contents will reflect the changes.

■**Tip** You may still wonder why it makes sense to create the table of contents now. The answer is simple. You can use the table of contents to navigate through your document because it is linked to the sections of the business proposal. Simply hold the mouse pointer over one of the entries in the table of contents. Then hold the Ctrl key and click the mouse. Word takes you to that section of your document.

To insert your table of contents, place the cursor at the beginning of the first line of your outline. Then click Insert ➤ Reference ➤ Index and Tables to bring up the Index and Tables dialog box. Open the Table of Contents tab, as shown in Figure 8-5.

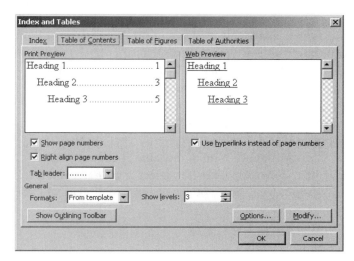

Figure 8-5. *The Table of Contents tab in the Index and Tables dialog box*

The Print Preview box will show you how the table of contents will appear in final form. Word will not show the actual headings in the Print Preview box. Rather, it shows the position of the different heading levels, substituting "Heading 1," "Heading 2," and so forth in place of headings.

Word has six predefined formats for you to choose. You can also opt to apply text formatting from the document template, which allows you to base the formatting on styles you specify.

The predefined formats will save you some time. However, they may not be appropriate for a business proposal. If you decide to use one, opt for the Classic format.

You are also able to change certain elements in the table of contents. You can alter the appearance of page numbers and leader lines and select how many levels the table of contents will contain.

With a professional document such as a business proposal, you should emphasize function over form. So design the table of contents with readability in mind.

Page numbers are a necessity, so make sure to select Show page numbers in the Index and Tables dialog box. You probably also want to select Right align page numbers, as this will give the table a clean, organized look.

If you align the page numbers along the right margin, you will do well to add tab leader lines, which will guide the reader's eye to the correct page number. Of course, Word provides a few different choices for how the leader lines appear. A dotted leader line is both unobtrusive and effective. Use the drop-down box to select the style you want.

■Note Switching between predefined formats may change the other options in the dialog box. So if you make a change, don't forget to reselect any options that have changed.

Finally, use the Show levels drop-down box to select how many heading levels to show. Moderation is best. However, you want your reader to find the relevant section easily.

When you've specified the options for the table, click OK. Your table of contents appears at the top of the document, above the document outline.

If you switch to Print Layout view, you will notice that the table of contents is on the same page as the outline. You will want to insert a page break between the table of contents and the rest of the business proposal.

To insert a page break, position the cursor at the end of the table of contents. Click Insert ➤ Break. In the Break dialog box, shown in Figure 8-6, select Page break and click OK. This ensures that the business proposal will begin on a new page. The break will not appear in Outline view.

Figure 8-6. *The Break dialog box*

As you work on the business proposal, Word may not update the page numbers or headings in the table of contents. This is normal. Word will make the appropriate changes when you print the document.

If it is important to you that the table of contents be updated as you work, you can tell Word to update it. On the Outlining toolbar, click Update TOC. The Update Table of Contents dialog box appears, as shown in Figure 8-7.

You will have two choices on what to update. Choose Update page numbers only if you only want to update the page numbers. If you've made changes to the headings, select Update entire table. Click OK.

Figure 8-7. *The Update Table of Contents dialog box*

Adding a Cover Page

Next, you should create a cover page for your business proposal. Position the cursor at the beginning of the first line of your outline. Enter the information you would like to appear on the cover page. Each line on the cover page should appear on its own line in Outline view.

Once you have entered the information for the cover page, you need to assign it to the correct level in the outline. Highlight the cover page information. Then on the Outlining toolbar, click the Outline Level drop-down box and select Body text.

Finally, you want to make sure the cover page information appears on its own page. Position the cursor at the end of the final line of the cover page. Click Insert ➤ Break. In the Break dialog box, select Page break and click OK. You will not see the page break in Outline view.

Entering the Main Body Text

Now you are ready for the main document. At this stage, you should enter text only. You will insert your charts, tables, and graphs later.

Also, avoid applying any formatting to the document. This includes bold, italics, and underlining. You do not want to use indentation yet, nor should you use the Tab key to indent text.

Right now, your primary concern is to enter the text data in your business proposal. You will apply formatting to paragraphs and text in one stage. This ensures that you will achieve clean, consistent formatting throughout the business proposal. You will use Word's style feature to apply the formatting, so Word will not retain manually applied formats.

Specifying Page Setup

Now you are ready to specify the page setup for the entire document. You may decide later to alter the page setup in specific parts of your business proposal. Or you may already know that the page setup will differ in certain areas. This is okay. For now, you are setting the predominant page layout for your business proposal.

Access the Page Setup dialog box by clicking File ➤ Page Setup. Click the Margins tab to open the settings for the margins, which you can see in Figure 8-8.

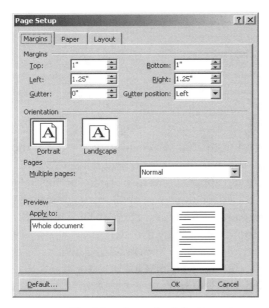

Figure 8-8. *The Margins tab of the Page Setup dialog box*

The default settings for the Normal.dot template are 1 inch at the top and bottom of the page and 1.25 inches at either side of the page. In most situations, these settings are appropriate for a business proposal. However, if you plan to bind the business proposal, you may want to increase the left margin by .25 inch. This ensures that the binding will not obstruct any of the printing.

▨**Caution** Avoid increasing the margins without a good reason, such as accommodating a binding. Otherwise, the margins will become distracting, and your business proposal may look insubstantial. Similarly, do not decrease the margins to fit more on the page. This will make the business proposal look cramped and difficult to read.

If you plan to add a header and footer, take that into consideration. Word will place the header and footer outside the margins you specify. You should also consider any footnotes you have added to the document.

The page orientation should be portrait. Also, check that the drop-down box labeled Pages reads Normal. The other options are not appropriate for a business proposal. In the drop-down box labeled Apply to, select Whole document.

Next, click the Paper tab, shown in Figure 8-9, in the Page Setup dialog box. In the Paper size section, use the drop-down box to specify the paper size; in this case, select the Letter size option, unless you must submit your business proposal on A4 or A6 paper.

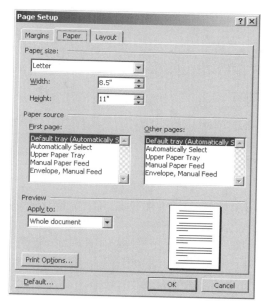

Figure 8-9. *The Paper tab of the Page Setup dialog box*

Use the boxes in the Paper source section to specify the printer's paper tray(s) for the first page of the business proposal and for the subsequent pages. In the Preview section, opt to apply the changes to the whole document.

Click the Print Options button to review the settings, as shown in Figure 8-10. Deselect Draft output if it has been selected. Select Update fields; this tells Word to check that the fields are current when the document prints. Similarly, select Update links. You should also select Drawing objects.

Once you have made your selections, click OK.

On the Layout tab, shown in Figure 8-11, check the document's vertical alignment. You want the text aligned to the top of the page, so select Top in the drop-down box. Once again, opt to apply the changes to the whole document. Click OK.

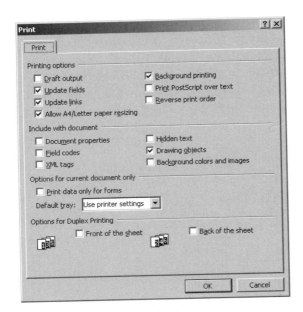

Figure 8-10. *The Print dialog box*

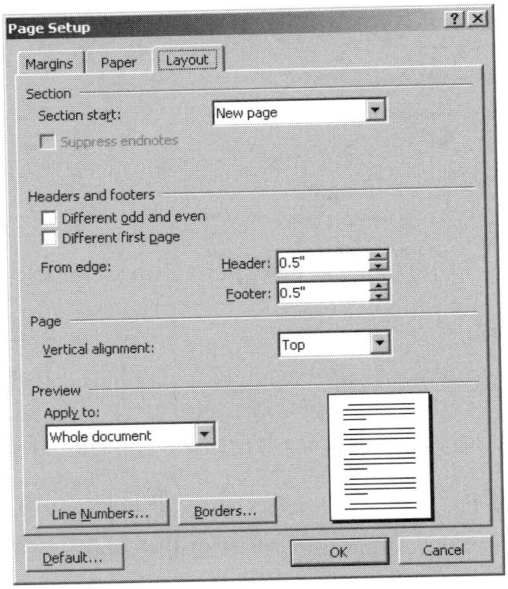

Figure 8-11. *The Layout tab of the Page Setup dialog box*

Formatting Your Business Proposal with Styles

When you're applying styles to your document, you have several tools that will help you. First, there is the Styles and Formatting task pane. To open it, click View ➤ Task Pane (or press Ctrl+F1). The task pane will appear in the right side of the Word window. Click the arrow at the top of the task pane and select Styles and Formatting. To open the Styles and Formatting task pane faster, simply click the Styles and Formatting button on the Formatting toolbar.

The Styles and Formatting task pane, which you can see in Figure 8-12, provides an easy way to create and apply styles. Once you select the portion of your document you would like to format, simply click a style in the task pane. Conveniently, the task pane identifies the section's current style.

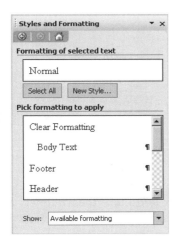

Figure 8-12. *The Styles and Formatting task pane showing the current style*

The Formatting toolbar also provides an easy way to check a selection's style and to apply styles. Simply select a portion of your document and use the Styles drop-down box to apply a style (see Figure 8-13). When you select a portion of your document, its style will appear in the Style box.

Figure 8-13. *The Style box on the Formatting toolbar*

You can also view applied styles at a glance by activating the Styles area. By default, Word hides the Styles area. But to activate it, click Tools ➤ Options and open the View tab, as shown in Figure 8-14. On the bottom of the tab, use the controls in the box labeled Style area width to specify the width for the Styles area. Click OK.

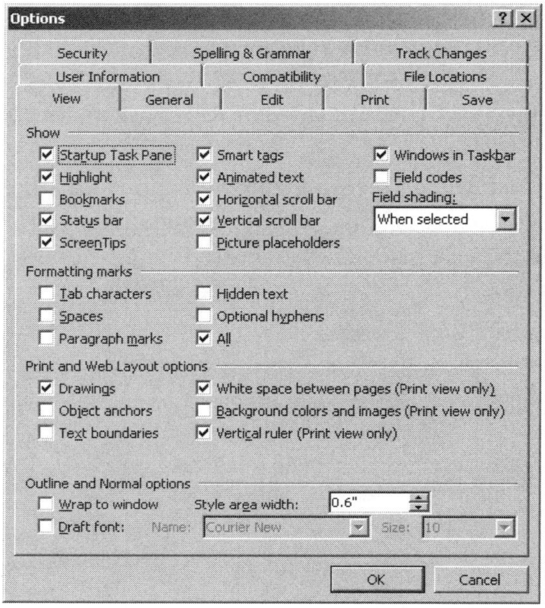

Figure 8-14. *The View tab of the Options dialog box*

The Styles area, shown in Figure 8-15, will appear along the left side of the window. A thin frame separates the Styles area from the rest of the document. You can click and drag the frame to increase or decrease the size of the Styles area.

Figure 8-15. *The Styles area*

■**Note** The Styles area does have limitations. First, you can only display it in Outline or Normal view. Second, it only shows styles applied to paragraphs. The Styles area will not display styles you apply to characters or portions of a paragraph. It is a handy feature, nonetheless.

You can also use the Styles area to change a paragraph's style. Double-click the style name in the Styles area. In the Style dialog box, shown in Figure 8-16, select the new style and then click Apply.

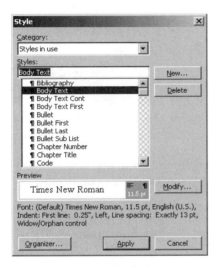

Figure 8-16. *The Style dialog box*

Word includes a variety of styles for you to use. But you may want to create your own styles. Fortunately, creating a style is not as difficult as you would assume.

The easiest way to create a style is to base it on a portion of the document. First, apply the formats you want to include in the style to part of your document. Paragraph styles can include character formatting such as bold, italics, underline, font color, and font size. Additionally, you can include alignment, margins, line spacing, and indents.

Once you have formatted the text, you have three options for defining the style. First, you can click in the Styles box on the Formatting toolbar and type a name for the style. Or, in the Styles and Formatting task pane, click the New Style button. Type a name for the style in the Name box and click OK (see Figure 8-17). Lastly, you can use the Styles area. Double-click the style name next to the formatted paragraph. In the Style dialog box, click New. Type a name for the style in the Name box and click OK.

Figure 8-17. *The New Style dialog box*

You can also create a style by specifying the formatting manually in the New Style dialog box. To access the New Style dialog box, click the New Style button on the Styles and Formatting task pane.

Enter a name for the style in the box labeled Name. Next, specify the type of style in the Style type box. You can select Paragraph, Character, Table, or List. Your choices will vary based on the type of style you create.

Use the controls to specify the formats to include in the style. If you don't see the options you need, click the Format button. As shown in Figure 8-18, a list pops up with more formatting options. The preview area shows you how the style will look.

Figure 8-18. *The Format list in the New Style dialog box*

You can tell Word to update the style when you make changes to text formatted with the style. Simply select Automatically update. When you have finalized your choices, click OK.

You can also create a new style based on an existing style. In the New Style dialog box, select the style you want to use in the drop-down list labeled Style based on.

■**Caution**   If you modify a base style, Word will update all styles you created from the base style. To avoid this, select (no style) in the box labeled Style based on in the New Style dialog box.

There is a good chance you will decide to modify a style you created. To do this, you need to access the Modify Style dialog box, as shown in Figure 8-19. In the Styles and Formatting task pane, hold the mouse over the style you would like to modify. Click the arrow that appears and select Modify. The Modify Style dialog box, which is similar to the New Style dialog box, will open.

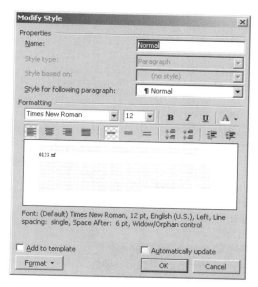

Figure 8-19. *The Modify Style dialog box is similar to the New Style dialog box.*

Alternatively, you can modify a style by formatting a portion of your document with the formats you would like to include in the style. Then hold the mouse over the style you would like to modify in the Styles and Formatting task pane. Click the arrow that appears and select Update to Match Selection.

■**Tip**   If you want to change all instances of a particular style, select a portion of the document formatted with the style. In the Styles and Formatting task pane, click the Select All button. Then click the new style you would like to apply. Also, you can delete all text formatted with the selected style by pressing Delete or Backspace.

Inserting a Table

Tables will play an important role in your business proposal. Use tables to organize data in balance sheets, sales projections, and other financials.

The easiest way for you to create a table in Word is to use the Insert Table button on the Standard toolbar.

Position the cursor where you would like the table inserted. Then click the Insert Table button. Use the drop-down grid to select the number of rows and columns for the table, as shown in Figure 8-20. When you release the mouse, Word inserts the table at the appropriate location in your document.

Figure 8-20. *Using the Insert Table button to create a table*

As Figure 8-21 demonstrates, tables you create with this method span the entire width of the document, no matter how many columns they contain.

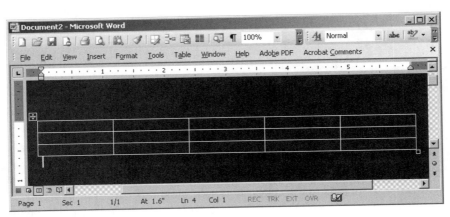

Figure 8-21. *A table created with the Insert Table button*

For more control over your columns, use the Insert Table dialog box, which allows you to specify a number of different formatting options for your table.

To access the Insert Table dialog box, place the cursor where you would like to position the table. Then click Table ➤ Insert ➤ Table. In the Insert Table dialog box, shown in Figure 8-22, specify the number of columns and rows you would like the table to contain. You can also set options for the column width. By default, Word automatically sets the width of the columns. However, you can use the Fixed column width box to specify the width of the columns in inches. Or, you can have Word AutoFit the table to the window or table contents.

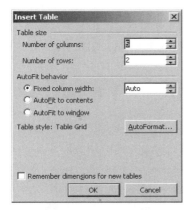

Figure 8-22. *The Insert Table dialog box*

Notice the AutoFormat button on the Insert Table dialog box. This opens a dialog box that allows you to specify predetermined formats to the table. In the Table AutoFormat box, shown in Figure 8-23, you first select a table style. Word displays the table formatting in the Preview box. At the bottom of the dialog box, you can use the selections to add or remove formatting from specific rows and columns. When you're done, click OK. Then click OK on the Insert Table dialog box.

To enter data in the table, simply click in a cell and begin typing.

If you decide you want to add more rows or columns to your table, you can do so quite easily. To add a row, click to the left of the row below which you would like to add a new row. Once the row is selected, the Insert Table button on the Standard toolbar changes to the Insert Rows button, as shown in Figure 8-24.

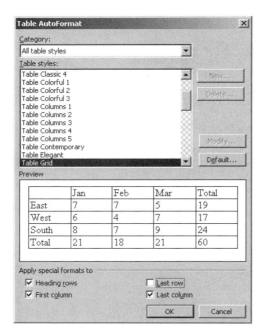

Figure 8-23. *The Table AutoFormat dialog box*

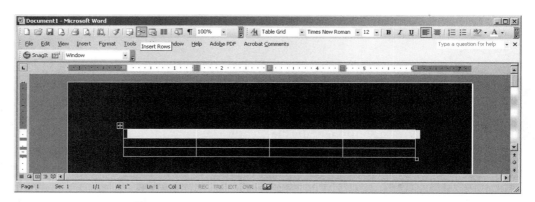

Figure 8-24. *Adding a row to a table*

To add a column, click the border above the column beside which you would like to insert an additional column. The Insert Table button on the Standard toolbar changes to the Insert Columns button, as shown in Figure 8-25. Word inserts the column to the left of the selected column.

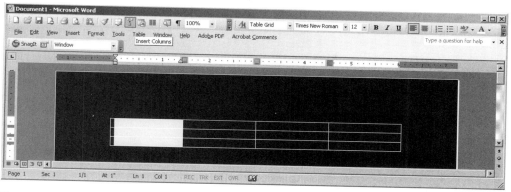

Figure 8-25. *Adding a column to a table*

■**Tip** For more flexibility in choosing where to insert rows and columns, use the Insert submenu on the Table menu instead of the toolbar buttons.

To remove rows or columns, select the row or column you would like to delete. Then click Table ➤ Delete and specify what to delete.

Modifying a Table's Layout

After you've created your table, you can make changes to the layout if you need. You can resize the columns and rows by clicking and dragging the borders. Also, you can merge or split cells as you would in Excel.

To merge cells, select the rows or columns you would like to combine. Then on the Table menu, click Merge Cells, as shown in Figure 8-26.

To split cells, select the row or column you would like to divide. Click Table ➤ Split Cells. In the Split Cells dialog box, shown in Figure 8-27, specify the number of rows or columns you would like to create. After you've specified the options, click OK.

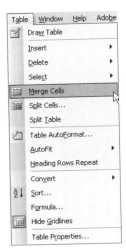

Figure 8-26. *Merging table cells*

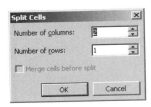

Figure 8-27. *The Split Cells dialog box*

Formatting Tables

If you didn't specify an AutoFormat when you created your table, or if you want to change the format you applied, you can still format your table.

To apply formatting to the characters in your table, select the text and use the buttons on the Formatting toolbar to change character attributes.

If you want to change text alignment, change table alignment, or apply borders and shading, you'll need to use the Table Properties dialog box, as shown in Figure 8-28. You can access this dialog box by selecting a portion of your table, right-clicking, and selecting Table Properties.

To change text alignment, open the Cell tab, shown in Figure 8-29, and specify text alignment properties. You can choose Top, Center, or Bottom. If you want to change text wrapping within cells, click the Options button. Specify whether you want text to wrap to the next line or to fit on one line. Click OK.

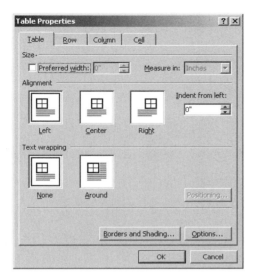

Figure 8-28. *The Table Properties dialog box*

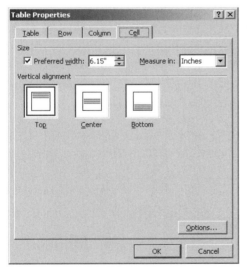

Figure 8-29. *The Cell tab of the Table Properties dialog box*

To change the table alignment, open the Table tab in the Table Properties dialog box, as shown in Figure 8-30. Select how you want Word to align the table on the page. For more control, you can specify a left indentation for the table.

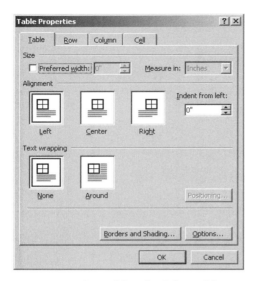

Figure 8-30. *The Table tab of the Table Properties dialog box*

You also have the option of wrapping document text around the table. For business proposals, you should turn text wrapping off.

You can specify margins for text within the cell and padding between the cells. This allows you to space your data nicely across the page. To access these controls, shown in Figure 8-31, click the Options button.

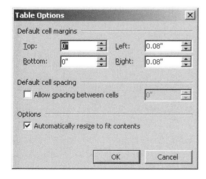

Figure 8-31. *Options for specifying cell margins and padding*

If you want to add borders or shading to cells, click the Borders and Shading button.

On the Borders tab, select the border style, color, and width (see Figure 8-32). There are border presets that will apply the border style you choose to specific areas of the table. Or, you can click in the diagram on the right to specify where you want the borders to appear.

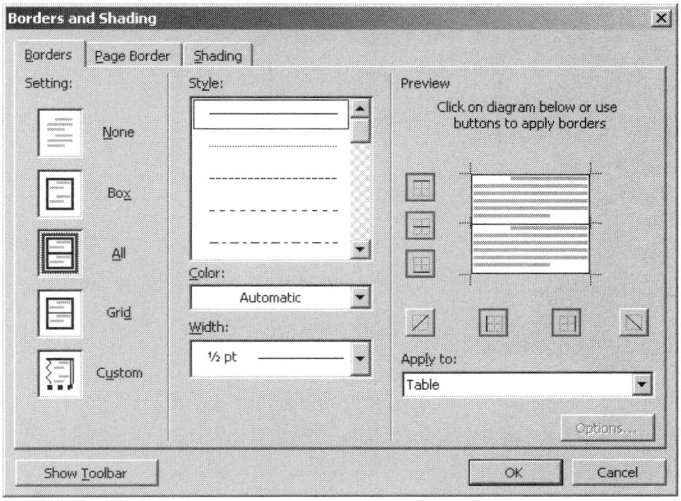

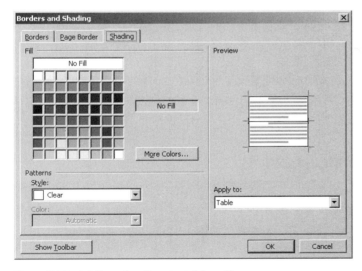

Figure 8-32. *Adding borders to a table*

To specify shading, open the Shading tab, as shown in Figure 8-33. Select the color you would like to apply from the color chart. For more options, click More Colors. In the Patterns sections, you can select a shading pattern. Finally, click OK.

Figure 8-33. *Adding shading to table cells*

To change a table that you've AutoFormatted, click in the table. Click Table ➤ Table AutoFormat. In the Table AutoFormat dialog box, click Modify. In the Modify Style dialog box, shown in Figure 8-34, enter a new name for the table style. Then use the controls to change the table formats. When you're done, click OK. Then close the Table AutoFormat dialog box.

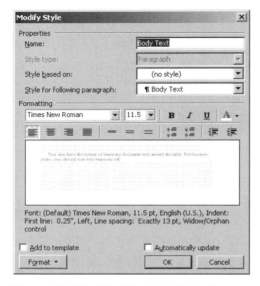

Figure 8-34. *The Modify Style dialog box*

Adding Captions to Your Tables

You may want to add a caption to your table, as it helps you identify the table when you refer to it in your business proposal.

To insert a caption, select your table. Click Insert ➤ Reference ➤ Caption to bring up the Caption dialog box, shown in Figure 8-35. In the Label box, select the type of label. Then specify the position of the label. Enter the caption text in the box labeled Caption.

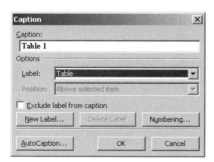

Figure 8-35. *The Caption dialog box*

Word inserts the caption as a field. The numbering updates automatically if you add more captions or rearrange captioned objects.

Creating Bulleted or Numbered Lists

There is a good chance that you will want to use bulleted or numbered lists in your document. These types of lists are notoriously difficult to work with in Word, although Word has significantly improved the way it handles lists.

Word generally tries to create a list if you begin a paragraph with a number or a symbol. When you end the paragraph by pressing Return or Enter, Word will AutoFormat the paragraph in a list style.

This AutoFormatting is frustrating for many users, particularly if a list is not desirable. And, if you have multiple paragraphs within a list item, it can be difficult to have Word format the list correctly.

I generally recommend that you disable lists in Word's AutoFormat section. This will alleviate much of the frustration. To do this, click Tools ➤ AutoCorrect Options. On the AutoFormat As You Type tab, shown in Figure 8-36, deselect Automatic bulleted lists and Automatic numbered lists.

Figure 8-36. *The AutoFormat As You Type tab of the AutoCorrect dialog box*

On the AutoFormat tab, shown in Figure 8-37, deselect Automatic bulleted lists and List styles. Click OK.

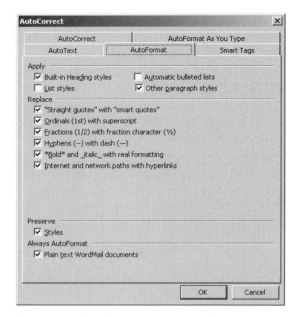

Figure 8-37. *The AutoFormat tab of the AutoCorrect dialog box*

Now you can create the lists as you like by inserting numbers or symbols for list items. Then you can adjust the indents as you want. For some, creating lists manually is preferable to messing around with Word's lists feature. However, keep in mind that lists won't automatically update when individual list items are moved or deleted.

But, for short lists, it is much easier to let Word create the list for you. To begin a list, simply click either the Bullets or Numbering button on the Formatting toolbar.

When you create a list using the toolbar buttons, it is best to allow Word to format the list automatically. Then if you want to make changes to the format, you can do so in one fell swoop when the list is complete.

To change the format of a bulleted list, double-click one of the bullet points. The Bullets and Numbering dialog box opens, as shown in Figure 8-38. There are a number of predefined list formats from which you can choose. Simply highlight one of the styles and click OK.

Or, you can customize a list style by clicking the Customize button. In the Customize Bulleted List dialog box, which you can see in Figure 8-39, you have a number of options. You can choose from one of the existing bullet characters by selecting it. Or, you can select a different symbol by clicking the Character button. The Font button allows you to change the bullet symbol's font.

In the Bullet position section, use the control box to select the indentation for the character. The Text position section changes the position of the text relative to the left margin. Tab space after sets the position of the first line of text. Indent at changes the position of all subsequent lines.

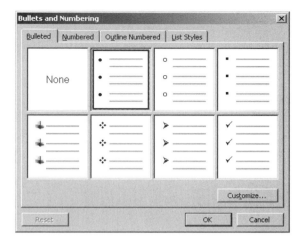

Figure 8-38. *The Bulleted tab of the Bullets and Numbering dialog box*

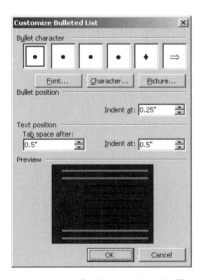

Figure 8-39. *The Customize Bulleted List dialog box*

Once you have made your changes, click OK in each of the open dialog boxes.

To change the formatting of a numbered list, double-click one of the numbers. The Bullets and Numbering dialog box will open (see Figure 8-40). Again, Word gives you the option of selecting from a predefined format for numbered lists on the Numbered tab. Select one and click OK to apply it. Or, you can click Customize to make changes.

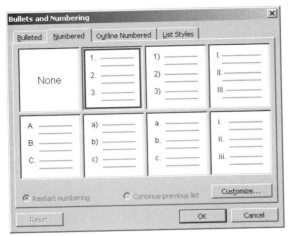

Figure 8-40. *The Numbered tab of the Bullets and Numbering dialog box*

In the Number format box of the Customize Numbered List dialog box, you can enter a number and a character, if you want a special format (see Figure 8-41). The Font button provides a way for you to change the font format for the list numbers. You can use the Number style box and the Start at box to apply a specific style of numbering and to change the number at which the list will start.

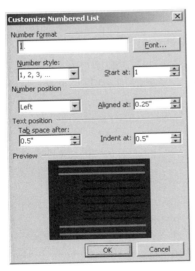

Figure 8-41. *The Customize Numbered List dialog box*

■Tip If you are continuing a previous list, don't use the Start at option to change the list. If you delete an earlier list item, the current list won't automatically update. Rather, use the Continue previous list option in the Bullets and Numbering dialog box.

In the Number position section, use the control box to select the indentation for the number. The Text position section changes the position of the text relative to the left margin. Tab space after sets the position of the first line of text. Indent at changes the position of all subsequent lines.

Once you have made your changes, click OK in each of the open dialog boxes.

If you want to remove a bullet point or number from a paragraph, simply position the cursor before the first character in the paragraph text. Then press the Backspace key. The bullet or number will be removed; the rest of the list updates automatically.

At the end of a list, press Enter or Return twice to turn off bullets and numbering and to return to a normal paragraph style.

Numbering Pages with Footers

You should add page numbers to your business proposal. Footers are ideal for listing page numbers—and any additional information.

Page numbers in the footer ensure that the business proposal can be reordered easily, should someone separate the pages. You should not number the cover page. However, if the table of contents runs over one page, you may want to number it.

To number the table of contents, place your cursor at the top of the first page. Click View ➤ Header and Footer. Click the Page Setup button on the Header and Footer toolbar to bring up the Page Setup dialog box shown in Figure 8-42. Use the controls to specify the distance from the edge of the paper. In the Preview section, select This point forward. Click OK.

Scroll down and click within the footer box. On the Formatting toolbar, click the Right Alignment button. Then on the Header and Footer toolbar, click the Insert Page Number button. Click the Format Page Number button. In the Page Number Format box, shown in Figure 8-43, select the number format. For a table of contents, use lowercase Roman numerals. Under Page numbering, select Start at and use the controls to select "i." Click OK.

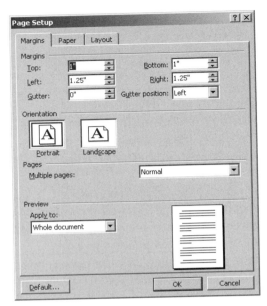

Figure 8-42. *The Page Setup dialog box*

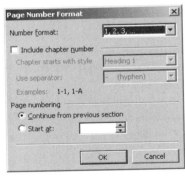

Figure 8-43. *The Page Number Format dialog box*

To add page numbers to the remainder of the business proposal, place your cursor at the top of the first page. Click View ➤ Header and Footer. Click the Page Setup button on the Header and Footer toolbar. Use the controls to specify the distance from the edge of the paper. In the Preview section, select This point forward. Click OK.

Scroll down and click within the footer box. On the Formatting toolbar, click the Right Alignment button. Then on the Header and Footer toolbar, click the Insert Page Number button. Click the Format Page Number button. In the Page Number Format box, select the number format. You should select standard numbering. Under Page numbering, select Start at and use the controls to select the appropriate page number. Click OK.

CHAPTER 9

■■■

Automating Document Creation

Templates go a long way to simplifying the document creation process. But Word offers other tools that will make the process even easier. You can use these tools on their own or in conjunction with templates.

Using Mail Merge to Complete Documents

Mail Merge is one of the easiest ways to automate the creation of documents. Mail Merge takes information from a data file and inserts it in a file that contains other text.

Mail Merge vs. Templates

At first blush, the difference between Mail Merge and templates may not seem terribly important. The goal of each is to simplify the document creation process.

But there is an important difference between the two. First, templates will ensure consistent formatting. They will even help you with standard text that appears in all documents created from a particular template.

On the other hand, Mail Merge aims to help you create multiple documents that contain the same text, but are customized for individual readers. Of course, adept users can add extra text to specific documents via the use of a field, but most users won't do this.

Templates and Mail Merge are not mutually exclusive. It is not uncommon to use a template as the main document for a Mail Merge operation: the template ensures that the text is formatted correctly, while the Mail Merge portion ensures that the correct text is entered.

Choosing a Data Source

You have a number of different options when it comes time to choose a data source for your Mail Merge. Word includes a built-in data source. You can also use contacts from Outlook or a table from an Access database. But perhaps the best source is an Excel spreadsheet.

It is easy to enter and arrange data in an Excel spreadsheet. Also, data can be imported to and exported from Excel. So here, you will use an Excel spreadsheet as an example.

Setting Up Mail Merge

Your data should be organized neatly into rows and columns. Think of each row as a single record and each column as a field you are going to insert into your document.

Create a header row for the sheet you intend to use for the Mail Merge. A *header row* is a row containing labels that identify the data in the cells below. Excel can be finicky sometimes about differentiating between data and labels, so provide clues: bold text, a cell border, and cell shading that are unique to the header row will ensure Excel differentiates it from the rest of your data.

Later, when you merge the data with the main document, the labels will appear as the names of the merge fields, so there will be no confusion as to what data you are inserting into your document. Furthermore, labeling your columns helps prevent user error.

The data you intend to use for the Mail Merge must be on one sheet. If it is spread across multiple sheets, you will need to combine the sheets or perform multiple Mail Merges. Also, make sure the sheets are clearly named, as you must select the sheet you intend to use without viewing it.

For the main document, you can use either a new, blank document, a template, or a document you've already created.

With the document open, activate the Mail Merge toolbar by right-clicking the gray space around the toolbars and selecting Mail Merge from the pop-up list.

On the Mail Merge toolbar, click the Main document setup button. In the Main Document Type dialog box, shown in Figure 9-1, select the type of document you wish to create. If you are unsure which to select, choose Letters, as this option will work for most types of documents. Then click OK.

Figure 9-1. *The Main Document Type dialog box*

Once you have created the main document, it is time to associate your data source with the document. On the Mail Merge toolbar, click the Open Data Source button.

When the Select Data Source dialog box appears, navigate through the folders until you find your Excel workbook (see Figure 9-2). If you are unable to find your Excel file, make sure you have selected All Data Sources in the drop-down box beside the Files of type label. When you find your file, open it by double-clicking it or by selecting it and then clicking Open.

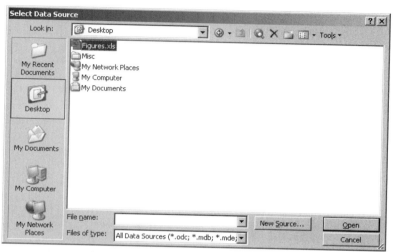

Figure 9-2. *The Select Data Source dialog box*

In the Select Table dialog box, shown in Figure 9-3, select the sheet that contains the data you wish to merge with your document. Before you click OK, make sure the box beside the option First row of data contains column headers is checked.

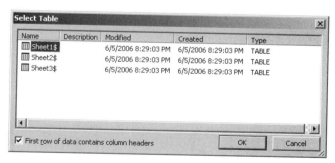

Figure 9-3. *The Select Table dialog box*

Now that the data source has been associated with the main document, you can begin entering text and/or editing your document. You cannot, however, make changes to your data source in Excel. If you need to make changes to the data, you must close the main document in Word before you can open the data source in Excel.

To insert merge fields into your document, click the Insert Merge Fields button on the Mail Merge toolbar. The Insert Merge Field dialog box will appear, as shown in Figure 9-4.

Figure 9-4. *The Insert Merge Field dialog box*

Highlight the name of the field you wish to insert from the list and click Insert. The box will stay open, allowing you to insert more fields. When you are done, click Close.

If you insert more than one field in succession, Word will not automatically add space between the fields in your document; you must do this yourself after you close the dialog box. In your document, you will see each field name surrounded by double arrows.

Microsoft recently added Mail Merge features that allow you to insert address blocks and greeting lines (see Figure 9-5). By clicking the respective button on the toolbar, Word will allow you to insert several fields at once, arranged in common variations.

Figure 9-5. *The Insert Block toolbar buttons*

Furthermore, when you click either button, Word displays a dialog box that gives you some options on which fields you would like inserted, how you would like them to be arranged, what punctuation to include, etc. (See Figure 9-6 for the dialog box that appears when you click the Insert Address Block button.) This is easy enough if you are using a data source created in Word, but it can get confusing if you are using an Excel worksheet.

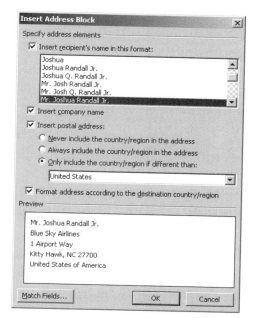

Figure 9-6. *The Insert Address Block dialog box*

Earlier I recommended that you use a header row in your worksheet. Well, if you named a field something other than what Word uses as a field name for similar data, Word might match the fields incorrectly.

This means if you use the Insert Address Block or Insert Greeting Line buttons, the data might appear in a different order than you specify—simply because the labels don't match. Fortunately, Microsoft anticipated this and built in a Match Fields feature that allows you to match your field names to the ones Word uses in the blocks.

To match fields, click the Match Fields button on the Mail Merge toolbar. In the Match Fields dialog box, shown in Figure 9-7, you will see a list of Word's field names on the left. On the right side of the box, you will see a column of drop-down boxes. The name in each drop-down box is the field that Word is using for each respective field in the Address Block or Greeting Line block. To make any changes, simply select the field name from the drop-down box. Once you are done making changes, click OK.

You can also bring up the Match Fields dialog box by clicking the Match Fields button at the bottom of either the Insert Address Block or Insert Greeting Line dialog boxes, both of which appear when you click the respective toolbar button.

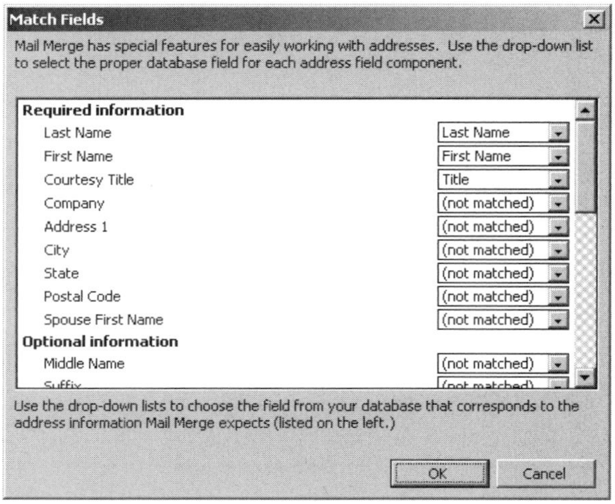

Figure 9-7. *The Match Fields dialog box*

To preview your merged documents, click the View Merged Data button on the Mail Merge toolbar (see Figure 9-8). This button works like a toggle switch, so if you want to go back to viewing just the fields and not the data they contain, click it again.

Figure 9-8. *The View Merged Data button*

You can navigate through the merged documents by using the navigational buttons on the Mail Merge toolbar, as shown in Figure 9-9. They are, from left to right, First Record, Previous Record, Go To Record, Next Record, and Last Record.

Figure 9-9. *The Mail Merge navigational buttons*

I recommend that before you merge your documents, you preview them all, or as many as you can, to verify that everything merged correctly—pay particular attention to things such as punctuation and spacing around the merged data.

■**Note** Word does not carry over the formatting of the data in the data source. If you want to apply special formatting such as italics, bold, or underline, you must do so in Word. If you are viewing the document with fields, you must select the double arrows on both sides of the field to which you want to apply the formatting. If you are viewing the merged data in the document, simply highlight the text you wish to change. Remember that any change will carry throughout all the merged documents, not just the individual one.

■**Tip** There is a way to have the merge fields appear exactly as they do in Excel, retaining the formatting of the Excel worksheet.

With the main document open, click the Tools menu and select Options. On the General tab, select Confirm Conversion at Open. Click OK.

When you select an alternative data source such as Excel, Word will ask you to choose the type of data source. When present with the choice, select MS Excel Files via DDE. The formatting from the worksheet will be carried over to the Word file.

Inserting Fields

Word also provides a number of different fields you can insert in your document. Unlike Mail Merge fields, Word determines the field values automatically or uses the field to perform an action. You probably already use fields in your document without realizing it. For example, Word uses field codes when you insert page numbers and create tables of contents.

To insert a field in your document, click Insert ➤ Field. In the Field dialog box, shown in Figure 9-10, you can use the Categories box to choose the type of field you would like to insert.

Depending on the type of field you are using, you will have a number of different options for the field. For example, with the Ask field, you can enter a prompt and a default response for the field. After you've specified the options for your field, click OK to insert it in your document. If you are unsure of a field's function, consult Word's Help feature by pressing F1.

Additionally, you can add arguments and switches to your fields. Because there are a variety you can add, and they largely depend on the field you're using, I won't cover them here. For more information, consult Word's Help feature.

Fields don't always automatically update. So, if you make changes that affect the contents of a field, the changes may not be apparent to you. In that case, you should update the field. To update a single field, select it and press F9. You can update all the fields in your document by pressing Ctrl+A to select the entire document and pressing F9 to update the fields.

Finally, you may wish to lock one or more fields in your document. To lock a field, select it and press Ctrl+F11. To unlock a field, press Ctrl+Shift+F11.

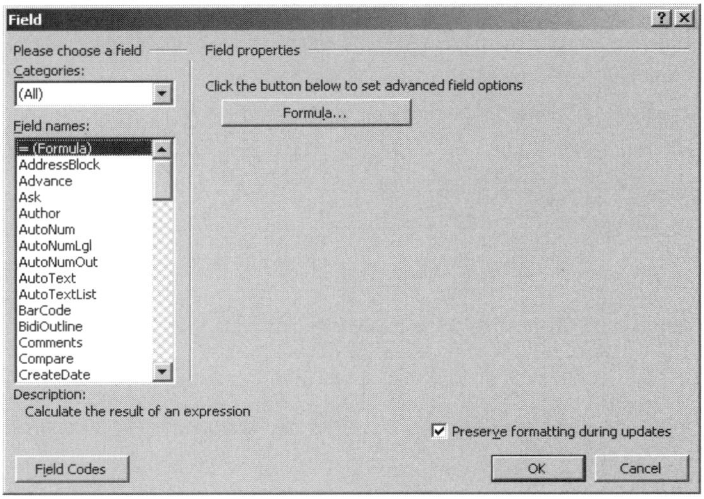

Figure 9-10. *The Field dialog box*

VIEWING FIELDS

When you insert a field in your document, you will see the contents of the field rather than the field code. But sometimes it is helpful to see the field code rather than its contents. To view the code for a single field, select the field and press Shift+F9. To show the codes for all the fields in the document, press Alt+F9. These hotkeys work as toggles.

You may also want to apply shading to the fields in your document. This will help you distinguish them easily from the rest of your document. To do so, click Tools ➤ Options. Open the View tab. In the drop-down box labeled Field shading, select Never, Always, or When selected. Click OK. With shading enabled, fields will contain a pale gray border on the computer screen.

AutoText

AutoText is an easy way to speed up the creation of your documents. You can automatically insert predefined text in parts of your document.

Using Preinstalled AutoText Entries

Word has a number of AutoText entries preinstalled that you can use. To access them, click Insert ➤ AutoText. On the submenu, you can select from a list of entries (see Figure 9-11). Click an entry, and Word automatically inserts it into your document.

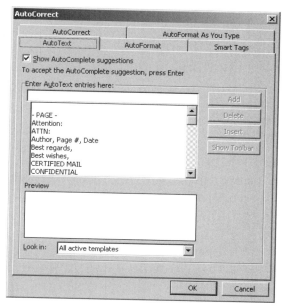

Figure 9-11. *The AutoText options tab of the AutoCorrect dialog box*

Tip The AutoText submenu detaches from the Insert menu. Click the dotted bar at the top of the menu and drag it into the document window. There, you now have easy access to the entries.

Defining Your Own AutoText Entries

By customizing AutoText entries, you can make creating documents even easier. To add AutoText entries, you must first open the Normal.dot template, the template upon which all Word documents are based.

The default location for the Normal.dot template in Windows XP is `C:\Documents and Settings\user name\Application Data\Microsoft\Templates`. Navigate to it via the Open dialog box in Word and open it.

Note If you try to open the Normal.dot template from Windows Explorer, a new, blank Word document will open, and you won't be able to make changes to the template.

To add your own AutoText entries, click Insert ➤ AutoText and select AutoText on the submenu. In the Box labeled Enter AutoText Entries here, type your AutoText entry (see Figure 9-12). Then click Add. Repeat for each entry you'd like to create. Once you're done, click OK.

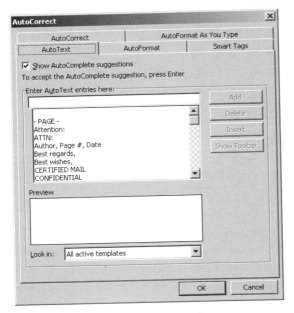

Figure 9-12. *Adding AutoText entries*

Save the Normal.dot template. To ensure the template is indeed saved as a template, select .dot in the drop-down box labeled Save as type in the Save As dialog box (see Figure 9-13).

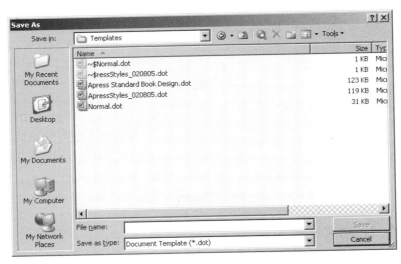

Figure 9-13. *Saving the Normal.dot template*

Now, you will be able to select your own custom text from the AutoText dialog box.

■ ■ ■

CHAPTER 10

Working with Large Documents

Long documents can be difficult to navigate and manage. Word's Outline view, as discussed in earlier chapters, makes it easy to create large documents. Fortunately, Word includes other tools that will help you create, review, and edit large documents. Many of these features also work well in a collaborative environment, where many people are working on the same document.

Using Word's Bookmark Feature

Word's Bookmark feature is a handy way to mark specific parts of your document. It enables you to return quickly to a marked location, rather than scroll through pages and pages of your document.

To insert a bookmark in your document, position the cursor at the location you would like to mark and click Insert ➤ Bookmark, or you may use the Ctrl+Shift+F5 keyboard shortcut.

In the Bookmark dialog box, shown in Figure 10-1, type a name for the bookmark. Click Add.

Note Bookmark names must start with a letter and cannot contain spaces. However, you can use an underscore to separate words. If you plan on inserting a number of bookmarks, a descriptive, easily distinguishable name is essential.

Figure 10-1. *The Bookmark dialog box*

To return to the bookmarked location, open the Bookmark dialog box from the Insert menu. Highlight the name of the bookmark and then click Go To.

Bookmarks are not visible in the finished document. However, if you do want to delete bookmarks, you can do so by highlighting them in the Bookmark dialog box and clicking Delete.

Working with Word's Reviewing Features

Word's reviewing features are a great way to keep track of the changes you've made to your document. These features also allow you to insert comments on particular portions of your document, which is handy in the editing and reviewing stages of your document.

Tracking Changes

When you're working on a long document, it is often valuable to track changes you make. This is particularly true if you are working with others on the same document.

Word's Track Changes feature allows you to not only see what changes you and others have made to the document, but also to accept or reject all or some of them. This is a powerful tool when it comes time to finalize the document.

Before you can take advantage of these options, you must first turn on the Track Changes feature by clicking Tools ➤ Track Changes. You can also double-click TRK on the status bar, use the Ctrl+Shift+E keyboard shortcut, or click the Track Changes button on the Reviewing toolbar (the Reviewing toolbar appears when Track Changes is enabled).

Note If you are working with others on the same document and want to track their changes, make sure they enable the Track Changes feature.

When Track Changes is enabled, the TRK button on the status bar changes from gray to black, as you see in Figure 10-2.

TRK

Figure 10-2. *The TRK button on the status bar*

Any additions or insertions you make in the document will appear in underlined, colored text (text color will vary depending on options you specify and/or which user makes the change). If you delete a portion of the document by hitting the Delete key or cut the text out of a paragraph, a balloon containing the deleted text will appear in the right margin with a dotted line connecting it to its original location in the document. Further-more, a vertical black line will appear in the left margin indicating where changes have been made.

You can turn off the Track Changes feature the same way you turn it on. Turning off the feature will not affect the changes that have already been tracked.

Word gives you the option of accepting or rejecting changes made to a document. This is helpful if you are working with others. Even if you aren't working with others, though, you may change your mind about a revision.

To accept one change in a document, click the change in the document or the Reviewing Pane. On the Reviewing toolbar, click the Accept Change button. To accept all changes within the document, click the arrow beside the Accept Change button and select Accept All Changes in Document, as shown in Figure 10-3.

Figure 10-3. *Accepting all changes in a document*

To reject a change, click the change in the document or the Reviewing Pane. On the Reviewing toolbar, click the Reject Change button. To reject all changes in the document, click the arrow beside the Reject Change button and select Reject All Changes in Document, as shown in Figure 10-4.

Figure 10-4. *Rejecting all changes in a document*

Inserting Comments

When working on long documents, Word's comments feature can be invaluable. It provides the ability to add notes and reminders within the document. If you are collaborating on a document, it is also handy for communicating with your collaborators.

You can easily hide, delete, or print notes inserted using the comments feature. Furthermore, when the comments are displayed onscreen, you can easily see the comments simply by scrolling through the document or by opening the Reviewing Pane.

To insert a comment, select the text upon which you would like to comment. Then click Insert ➤ Comment or click the New Comment button, shown in Figure 10-5, on the Reviewing toolbar. A balloon will appear in the right margin. Type your comment in the balloon. You can then click anywhere in the document to continue editing it.

Figure 10-5. *The New Comment button*

The text you selected will have red lines surrounding it, and a dotted red line will connect it to the comment balloon.

To delete a comment, simply right-click the balloon and select Delete Comment.

■**Caution** Before you share a finalized document electronically, you probably want to delete all the comments in your document. You can do this by clicking the arrow beside the Reject Change button on the Reviewing toolbar and selecting Delete All Comments in Document.

When using Word's reviewing features, you have different options for viewing comments and revisions. Word displays the changes in markup balloons in the right margin of the document and/or in the Reviewing Pane at the bottom of the Word window.

To have comments or changes appear in balloons, click Show on the Track Changes toolbar. On the Balloons submenu, click Always or Only for Comments/Formatting (see Figure 10-6).

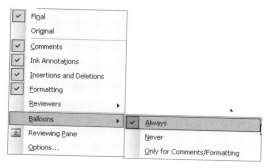

Figure 10-6. *Selecting view options for tracked changes*

To display the Reviewing Pane, click Show on the Track Changes toolbar and select Reviewing Pane or click the Reviewing Pane button on the Track Changes toolbar.

Working with Document Versions

You may find it helpful to keep a history of the versions of your document. Word's Versions feature allows you to keep different versions of the document within the same file. You won't have multiple files to sort through, and it saves disk space.

At any time, you can save the current version of your document manually. Simply click File ➤ Versions. In the Versions dialog box, shown in Figure 10-7, click Save Now.

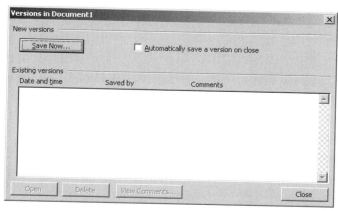

Figure 10-7. *The Versions dialog box*

The Save Version dialog box opens, as shown in Figure 10-8, allowing you to add comments on the document version. Once you have entered any comments, click OK and Close. The next time you open the Versions dialog box, the version you saved will appear.

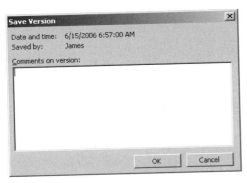

Figure 10-8. *The Save Version dialog box*

You can also have Word automatically store versions when you close a document. Click File ➤ Versions. In the Versions dialog box, select Automatically save a version on close. Click Close.

When you store a version of your document using the Versions feature, you can access previous versions, delete any of the versions stored with your document, and recover document versions to a new file.

To view a different document version, click File ➤ Versions. In the Versions dialog box, highlight the version you would like to view and click Open.

The version will open in a new window, tiled horizontally beneath the current document window. You can scroll through your document and interact with it as you would a normal document.

While you can make changes to the version of the document, you cannot alter the stored version of the document. If you do make changes to the document, it must be stored under a new file name.

To delete a version of your document, highlight the version in the Versions dialog box. Click Delete. In the pop-up box, click Yes to confirm the deletion. Click Close.

■Caution Deleting previous versions of your document is important if you intend to share it with other users, as they will be able to view any versions included with electronic copies of your documents.

Using Word's Master Document Feature

Word's Master Document feature is a handy way to manage large documents, such as a book with many chapters. This is particularly true if you are collaborating on the document. The Master Document is essentially a container for a number of different files, which are referred to as subdocuments.

Before you start a Master Document, you should create a folder that will contain the Master Document and all the subdocuments. If you already have some of the subdocuments created, move them to the folder.

You can create a Master Document from scratch or convert an existing document to a Master Document.

To create a Master Document from scratch, open a new blank document in Outline view. Then create headlines. Each headline will become a subdocument. If you want to add a title for the document, put it as a top-level heading. Then put the subdocuments as Level 2 headings.

To convert an existing document to a Master Document, open the document and view it in Outline view. Use the buttons on the Outlining toolbar to add heading levels to parts of the document. Again, use Heading 1 for the title and Heading 2 for the subdocuments. Demote any other content to body text by using the buttons on the Outlining toolbar.

To convert the document to a Master Document, you must first create subdocuments, as described in the next section.

Creating Subdocuments

You can create a subdocument from an outline heading in your Master Document. Open the Master Document and select the headings and body text you would like to separate into subdocuments.

Note The first heading you select must be the same level as the headings you want to use for each subdocument. For example, if you use Heading 2 as the first subdocument, each part of the document at Level 2 will be converted to a new subdocument.

On the Outlining toolbar, click Create Subdocument (see Figure 10-9). Once you create a subdocument, do not move it or delete it from your hard drive without first removing it from the Master Document. Only rename subdocuments from within the Master Document.

Figure 10-9. *The Create Subdocument button*

Adding an Existing Document to the Master Document

Open the Master Document in Outline view. Click Expand Subdocuments (see Figure 10-10) on the Outlining toolbar if the subdocuments are collapsed.

Figure 10-10. *The Expand Subdocuments button*

Click a blank line between existing subdocuments where you want to add the existing document. Then click Insert Subdocument on the Outlining toolbar (see Figure 10-11). Type the name of the document you wish to add in the file name box and click Open.

Figure 10-11. *The Insert Subdocument button*

Saving the Master Document

Save the Master Document as you would any other Word document. Make sure you save it in the folder you created for the Master Document and subdocuments.

Word will save the Master Document and create subdocuments with titles based on the subdocuments' headings in the Master Document outline.

Collapsing Subdocuments

When you're working with your Master Document, you may not want to see the contents of the subdocuments. In that case, you can collapse subdocuments by clicking Collapse Subdocuments on the Outlining toolbar (see Figure 10-12).

Figure 10-12. *The Collapse Subdocuments button*

■**Caution** If you are collaborating with others, collapse the subdocuments before you close the Master Document. Otherwise, others will not be able to access the subdocuments.

Combining Subdocuments

To combine subdocuments, you must first make sure you can see the subdocuments you want to combine. Ensure they are unlocked. If they are not, click within each locked subdocument and then click the Lock Subdocuments button on the Outlining toolbar (see Figure 10-13).

Figure 10-13. *The Lock Subdocuments button*

The subdocuments should be next to each other. If they aren't, rearrange them. To move a subdocument, click the subdocument icon, or for multiple subdocuments, hold the Shift key as you click the subdocument icon for the last of the adjacent subdocuments (see Figure 10-14). Then drag the subdocument(s) to a new location.

Figure 10-14. *The Insert Subdocument button*

Next, click the subdocument icon of the first document you want to combine. Hold down the Shift key as you click the subdocument icon of the final subdocument you wish to combine. On the Outlining toolbar, click Merge Subdocument (see Figure 10-15).

Figure 10-15. *The Merge Subdocument button*

Word will save the subdocuments under the file name of the first subdocument. The original versions of the other subdocument files will remain in the folder containing the Master Document and subdocuments.

■**Tip** You can move text, pictures, and other elements between subdocuments. First, expand the subdocuments. Then switch to Print Layout view (View ➤ Print Layout). You can then move elements as you would in any other Word document.

Splitting a Subdocument into Two Subdocuments

To split a subdocument into two subdocuments, add a new heading for the new subdocument. You should format it with the same heading style used for the other subdocuments. Then on the Outlining toolbar, click Split Subdocument (see Figure 10-16). When you save the Master Document, Word will create a new subdocument with a name based on the subdocument heading in the Master Document.

Figure 10-16. *The Split Subdocument button*

■**Note** Sometimes Word automatically locks subdocuments. For example, if the subdocuments are collapsed or if someone else is currently working on the subdocument, Word will lock it. In most cases, you can unlock the subdocument by expanding the subdocument. If that does not unlock it, click Lock Document on the Outlining toolbar.

Printing a Master Document

The fastest way to print your subdocuments is to print the Master Document. But there are a few tricks to printing your Master Document.

First, open the Master Document in Outline view. Then click Expand the subdocuments to expand the subdocuments. You can expand or collapse the headings to display the portions of the document you wish to print.

The Outlining toolbar gives you a number of options for what to display. Only the portions you have set to display will print when you print your document.

Once you have made your selections, click Print on the Standard toolbar.

■**Tip** You can open a subdocument from within a Master Document. To do this, expand the subdocuments. Then double-click the subdocument icon. If the subdocument is locked, unlock it by clicking Lock Document on the Outlining toolbar.

Index

You Need the Companion eBook

Your purchase of this book entitles you to buy the companion PDF-version eBook for only $10. Take the weightless companion with you anywhere.

We believe this Apress title will prove so indispensable that you'll want to carry it with you everywhere, which is why we are offering the companion eBook (in PDF format) for $10 to customers who purchase this book now. Convenient and fully searchable, the PDF version of any content-rich, page-heavy Apress book makes a valuable addition to your programming library. You can easily find and copy code—or perform examples by quickly toggling between instructions and the application. Even simultaneously tackling a donut, diet soda, and complex code becomes simplified with hands-free eBooks!

Once you purchase your book, getting the $10 companion eBook is simple:

❶ Visit **www.apress.com/promo/tendollars/**.

❷ Complete a basic registration form to receive a randomly generated question about this title.

❸ Answer the question correctly in 60 seconds, and you will receive a promotional code to redeem for the $10.00 eBook.

2560 Ninth Street • Suite 219 • Berkeley, CA 94710

eBookshop